# FUEL FOR LIFE

## LEVEL-10 ENERGY

FIVE STEPS TO SUCCESS

# FUEL FOR LIFE

## LEVEL-10 ENERGY

FIVE STEPS TO SUCCESS

Gary R. Epler, M.D.

EPLER HEALTH

Epler, Gary R.
Fuel for Life: Level-10 Energy
Five Steps to Success

Library of Congress Control Number: 2013913872
ISBN:978-0-9849335-5-6



The views expressed in this publication are those of the author and do not necessarily reflect views of any medical group or of the staff, officers, or directors of Epler Health, Inc. This publication is for general informational purposes only, and it is not a substitute for professional medical advice. This publication does not offer a medical opinion about any specific facts. Competent medical advice should be sought before any action is taken in a specific situation by a particular party.

Printed in the United States of America

Other books by Gary Epler:
*You're the Boss: Manage Your Disease*
*BOOP: You're the Boss*
*Asthma: You're the Boss*
*Food: You're the Boss*

*This book is dedicated to people everywhere who know how to live at Level-10 Energy.*

*And to*

*My beautiful wife, Joan, who knows how to live every day filled with energy and excitement, and my two sons Greg and Brett, who taught us how.*

# Acknowledgments

**My thanks** to Dr. David P. White, Director, Sleep Disorders Program, Brigham and Women's Hospital in Boston, for his outstanding academic contribution about sleep. Thanks to Scott Molgard for his unwavering enthusiasm for the benefit of exercise, and to Tim Regan for his positive approach to the day. Thanks to Professor Randall Bartlett at Smith College for insights into thinking like an economist, to Professor Benjamin Schumacher at Kenyon College and Professor Sean Carroll of California Institute of Technology for their insights into quantum physics, to Professor Robert Sapolsky of Stanford University for his insights into neurobiology and behavior. Thanks to Stuart Wilde for his spiritual insights about money. Thanks to Deepak Chopra for his insights into universal energy, aging, and the power of the body to heal itself. Thanks to Mark Leary, Professor of Psychology and Neuroscience at Duke University, for his insight into happiness and stress. Thanks to Professor C. Nathan DeWall from the University of Kentucky for his insights into self-control and to Professor H. Craig Heller at Stanford University for his insights into sleep science. Thanks to Tim Ferriss for his endless energy to learn and to Michael Stone for his unwavering support of Level-10 Energy. Thanks to Glenda Garland for her interviewing journalism. And, finally thanks to Laurie Gibson and Karah Madrone for the meticulous editing and to Marian Ferro for her unerring proofreading.

# Contents

# 1

# Creating a Level-10 Energy Day

**Do you want to know** how to have the feeling of a high-energy day, every day? It's called a Level-10 Energy Day and it's extraordinary.

It's one of those days you love to have – everything goes well, you're on top of the world, nothing bothers you, you can accomplish anything! You're alive with energy. You're alert. Your eyes are open. You move. Your mind is working. You don't see problems. You see solutions. Your mind is generating positive thoughts. You talk to people. People talk to you. You listen to people. People listen to you. You make money. You're energized by your work. You help people. People help you. Little annoyances don't bother you. You're forgiving. You're grateful. Your senses are engaged. You hear the birds. You see the flowers. You feel the softness. You smell the sweet perfume. You taste food. You're creative. You enjoy life.

How do you have a Level-10 Energy Day? Begin with a positive approach to the day and follow these five steps.

- Get eight hours of sleep every night for recharging your brain.
- Do one hour of vigorous exercise at the best of your ability.
- Eat the three foods that will give you energy.
- Learn something new every day.
- Engage your mind by using alpha and theta brainwaves.

I first thought about a Level-10 Energy Day when my wife, Joan, and I were in central Australia several years ago. We were returning to our hotel and noticed a couple of men sitting on the curb. They looked like they'd been drinking alcohol day and night, probably for a very long time. They hung their heads, complaining about their gloomy lives, swaying back and forth in a level-1 energy stupor. I asked Joan if she thought they knew what a Level-10 Energy day felt like. She replied, "Probably not, at least not for a very, very long time." Which is ironic because they used alcohol at the beginning to give themselves a high-energy day, but instead they had a low-energy life, and seemed barely capable of sustaining existence.

I realized how fortunate Joan and I are to live Level-10 Energy Days. They're exhilarating! You create so much energy that you can accomplish anything, and you feel great doing it.

So what is Level-10 Energy? My theory is that this is the hologram energy of the universe. A hologram is a three-dimensional image of an object or person that has a special property: you can cut it in half, and it's still whole. You can cut it into tiny pieces, and each piece contains the whole image. There is a final packet of energy that still contains the whole image, and taken from quantum physics, this packet of energy contains everything that has ever happened since the beginning of the universe, everything that's going on at this moment, and everything that will happen in the future.

Level-10 Energy is the melding together of these subatomic, each identical packets of energy available to you at all times.

What is the relationship between this special energy and a Level-10 Energy Day? It's one of several types of energy used for creating these wonderful days. The other energies include adenosine energy during sleep, muscle energy during exercise, and food energy from proteins, omega-3 fatty acids, and slow-burn carbohydrates. Level-10 Energy is especially helpful during exercise, learning something new, and during waking alpha and theta brainwave states.

You've used Level-10 Energy all your life, usually at the subconscious level. You know you're using Level-10 Energy when you connect and work with the people you are meant to serve, when you're doing something that is intrinsically important to you and has meaning, and when you're doing things worth getting excited about. Someone who is wallowing in self-pity and complaining about life is using level-1 or level-3 energy, not nearly enough to bring excitement, vitality, and bliss into daily life.

My friend Michael Stone knows Level-10 Energy. For years he struggled to get his business off the ground. He was clear on who he wanted to serve and how he wanted to serve them, yet he struggled to define a clear and attractive value proposition. In less than six months of using Level-10 Energy, he was on his way to building a successful consulting, speaking, and coaching business. Now, his vision, message, and output are clear and concise. In the last two years he has written two books and is writing a third. Instead of employees, he created a team of partners who helped him achieve his goals and further his message. The interaction of these partners helped his clients and customers succeed with their goals. This is Level-10 Energy at work: it brought these partners to Mike and in turn, they used it to help him and his customers attain valuable results.

You're surrounded by sources of Level-10 Energy everywhere, including social interactions, your job, your community, and music. Find your own sources.

This chapter will present the general approach to creating a Level-10 Energy Day, every day.

Let's begin with the understanding that you need to take an active, fully aware approach to the day. A traditional approach has been to passively go through the day dealing with problems as they develop, experiencing haphazard sleep with too little most nights and too much on weekends, taking no exercise, randomly eating all types of food without awareness, and neglecting mind-body introspection. This is a recipe for disaster leading to level-3 day or at most a level-5 day.

A successful Level-10 Energy Day involves actively taking charge and managing the day with energy. Start the day with gratitude for the opportunity to have an exciting day. Start the morning with anticipation – this is going to be a great day! Expect a great day.

Use my friend, Tim Regan's experience to your benefit. I work out with him every morning, and he told me that his dad used to wake him up with "Get up! Get up! This could be the best day of your life!" Tim truly believes that every day has the possibility of being the best day of his life. That's the way to start your day. Tim is astonishingly successful, an intense "tough mudder" competitor, and when someone asks him how his day is going, he says, "Terrific, and getting better!"

Train your mind to have positive thoughts. Make someone's day better by saying something nice to that person.

---

Jeb begins his day complaining about having to get out of bed. He goes through the motions of shaving and brushing his teeth. Before going to work, he has a cup of coffee and a bagel with cream cheese. He complains about the traffic on the way to work and yells at a driver who cut in front of him. After a perfunctory, grumpy hello to his coworkers, he begins his job and dreads every part of it, waiting for the end of the day. He eats a muffin during his 10 o'clock break, and complains about eating muffins because they make him fat, and then he has another one. At lunch, he orders two burgers, fries, and a shake from a local fast-food drive-through. He has a drink with his friends after work, and they complain about their terrible bosses, fellow workers, and politicians. They share their anger at the rival sports teams and the incompetent coaching of the home teams. Jeb eats dinner with his family and complains about the school and the children's homework. He watches the news and falls asleep during his favorite TV show. He goes to bed after midnight and starts the next day at 7 a.m., repeating the same pattern.

---

Whoa, that's a hard story to finish! It's boring and chock-full of enough complaints to make someone stop reading this book. What you just saw was a level-5 day and, sadly, it's a typical day for too many people. But keep reading and soon you'll learn how to create and experience Level-10 Energy Days. Let's find out from Jenn. She knows.

---

Jenn is up at 6 o'clock after going to bed at 10 p.m. She heads to her workout club where she runs a mile on the treadmill at a good pace for aerobic conditioning and then does some interval 400s to get her muscles firing. She goes to the step aerobics class where Liv has saved a step for her at her favorite spot. The instructor is upbeat and the music is great. She drinks a bottle of water during her workout. After a shower, she's at her Level-10 Energy pace and is excited to start the day. She has a small orange juice and a protein breakfast. At work she creates and organizes a new project with enthusiasm and success. Her lunch is creative with thin-sliced boiled chicken and avocado mixed with lemon and some olive oil sprinkled on top. Jenn has a radio show in the afternoon that's enjoyable and a huge success. She finishes the day with her husband and kids, riding the bike path through the hills.

That's a Level-10 Energy Day! And, the next day is going to be new and filled with new energy, creativity, and enjoyment.

---

Which of the two stories above applies to you? Jeb, the extreme example of a level-5 energy day? Or Jenn, with her exciting Level-10 Energy Day? Are you somewhere in between?

Jeb did everything wrong. He had a terrible sleep pattern: too little sleep during the night and falling asleep while watching TV. He had no exercise routine and avoided any extra exertion during the day. He complained incessantly, focusing his attention on negative things over which he had no direct control. He spread his negative thinking and complaining to his family. He didn't think about seeing the good in anything around him like the remarkably gifted teachers at his children's school. He didn't learn to enjoy his work or to make an effort to promote himself to create an enjoyable job. His eating was random which set him up for being overweight and developing diabetes, hypertension, and heart disease. This may be an extreme example, but too many people have too many of these level-5 energy days.

Jenn took the wise approach. She had eight hours of sleep, then made the effort to do an hour of vigorous exercise. She chose to see her day with a positive attitude and also made sure to eat the type of foods that continued to give her high energy into the evening.

How do you take charge of your day? Follow the five vital steps. Begin with the first one. Sleep eight hours every night. Although the mind needs no sleep, your brain does. It needs to be recharged every day. Eight hours is needed to replace adenosine, the energy chemical, and restore the brain glycogen supply, six hours is not enough and ten hours is too much.

After sleep, follow the second step. Exercise vigorously for one hour. This is at the best of your ability. Exercise gives you energy. The heart and lungs bring oxygen and nutrients to cells and carry away toxins. The brain responds by increasing your energy level and releasing feel-good neurotransmitters like endorphins, dopamine, and serotonin. Group exercise also increases oxytocin, the human bonding hormone. Exercise decreases stress.

The third step is to eat the right foods in the right amount. The three groups of energy-producing foods are lean protein, omega-3 fatty acids, and slow-burn carbohydrates. Be aware of what you eat and take advantage of the natural rhythms of eating three times daily.

Step four is constant learning, learn something new every day. People may not like to study and take tests, but everyone loves to learn. It gives you energy, creativity, and enjoyment. You'll learn something to help someone. You'll learn something to improve your life.

You have now reached the final step for creating your Level-10 Energy Day, which is to use the power of your mind. There are several ways to do this. First, engage your mind by using alpha and theta brainwaves, the alpha brainwaves for creativity and the theta brainwaves for healing. Second, use visualization by reprogramming your cells for renewal of healthy, strong growth. Third, use compassion. It's comforting and gives you energy. Fourth, use controlled breathing. Our bodies have an endless energy-based system that can be used to heal and provide energy throughout the day.

---

Before beginning the next chapter, let me introduce you to Dave and Kate. They're wonderful people. When they first met, they were both upbeat and full of life, filled with excitement and big dreams. Yet, gradually over time, they drifted into average level-5 energy lives. Random events began to happen. There was a fender bender. Kate was given a warning by the police because she came to a rolling stop at an intersection. Dave's safety sticker expired. A tree fell on their house during a freaky ten-minute windstorm. The sink was plugged and the shower leaked. These are large and small annoyances that happen in life, yet the couple dwelled on them and complained about them constantly.

For Dave, there was no new creative or challenging change in his job. Kate no longer had the excitement of going to work. They enjoyed watching their favorite TV shows at night with a snack, but often they both dozed off, so they went to bed late, resulting in a restless night of interrupted sleep. They both felt gloomy when they woke up and went to work.

Little things annoyed them throughout the day, and they sometimes snapped at each other. They enjoyed seeing their friends, and had phenomenal vacations, but after a few years they stopped skiing and going on their weekly hikes. Their dreams were smaller now, just getting through the workday and returning home was their usual goal.

Sounds like Dave and Kate are depressed, doesn't it? These are indeed some symptoms of depression, but Dave and Kate are not actually in need of psychiatric help, and they have a good marriage. But they've drifted into typical, average level-5 energy days.

Dave and Kate heard about Level-10 Energy and made some changes in hopes of making a difference in the quality of their lives. We'll find out what they did, and how you can start living and leading an enjoyable, creative Level-10 Energy life, every day.

---

In the next chapters, each of the five vital steps will be discussed in detail. You'll learn to live a Level-10 Energy Day, every day.

# 2

# Your Brain Can't Live Without Its Required Hours of Sleep

**For the first step,** it's important that you learn everything you can about the value of sleep. Read and listen to research about it, and use your own body to feel its benefits. This is what you'll find: you need eight hours of sleep every day, not less and not more.

Why?

The function of sleep remained a mystery for centuries, but now, we have begun to find some answers, or at least to develop some theories to unravel the unrivaled need for sleep.

Simply stated, sleep recharges the brain, and it takes eight hours to do this.

—

Mark put his laptop down on his cubicle desk with a thump and an angry sigh.

"Was it rough in there?" his friend Jeff asked from a nearby desk. Jeff knew Mark had just given a presentation to their boss.

"Brutal," Mark said. "They asked me question after question, way too quickly, and it was clear they think I hadn't thought the whole thing through, which is crazy. I worked hard staying up late for the past three nights getting ready for this."

"And thanks for helping me after I ran in here late," he added.

"No problem," Jeff said. "What happened, by the way? You oversleep?"

"I fell asleep on the train and missed the stop. Then I had to wait for another train going in the other direction."

"That's happened to everyone, I'm sure," Jeff said, although it had never happened to him.

Mark shuffled around some papers, knocking a few off his desk. "And it'll probably happen again tomorrow, too, because I've got to figure out how to make this project work. I'll be up all night again," he said, angrily.

"Try some sleep, it'll give you energy to finish the project," Jeff said without trying to lecture his friend.

"Who has time?"

"Who doesn't is the better question. Sleep is important. Healthy sleep allows you to come up with good ideas, boosts your mood, and gives you the energy to tackle all the things they," Jeff pointed toward the conference room, "toss at you."

Mark sat down heavily. "I've never needed a lot of sleep. I can fall asleep in two minutes any time I want and any place."

"That's actually not a good thing. You just flunked the five-minute sleep test – you're chronically sleep-deprived," Jeff said. He turned to his computer. "Here, I'll send you some links about why we need to get enough sleep. You decide."

---

The way Mark thinks about sleep is all too common. There is so much competing for our attention and time that sleep can seem like a waste of time. But when you learn about sleep, everything will point to and reinforce the idea that a person needs eight hours of sleep a day, not more and not less.

Performance tests have determined that cognitive abilities like memory formation and concentration decrease markedly when people get less than seven hours of sleep a night. During sleep, the brain forms and reinforces memories of tasks learned. Without adequate sleep, it takes longer to learn and remember.

The ability to concentrate, focus, and stay on task suffers with too little sleep. Researchers call this "ability vigilance" and test it by asking a person to press a button when a light dot randomly appears on a screen. The test focuses on measuring how many times the person realizes the dot is there and presses the button, assessing how often the person's attention stays on the screen or strays from it. A person with less than seven hours of sleep performs much worse on the vigilance test than someone who slept for eight hours. For a person who has six hours of sleep or less a day, a much greater number of dots are missed, and if that pattern is maintained for two weeks, the scores will continue to decline.

Worse, creativity is lost and the person is not aware of it. We all know that after a night of little, no, or very poor sleep, we can get grumpy. But, the sleep deprivation of having six hours of sleep or less per day gives a person a new sense of "normal." In this state, a person might not make the best choices, from what foods to eat for lunch, to arguing with a spouse over a minor annoyance, to taking a curve at 50 mph instead of the recommended 25.

If this description sounds like someone who has been drinking too much alcohol, you're right. Researchers have compared sleep deprivation to alcohol intoxication levels and found a direct correlation – the more sleep deprived a person is, the stronger that person compares to someone with an increased blood alcohol level.

Most of our jobs don't require that we concentrate all the time, so they don't provide feedback about whether we've entered a period of consistent sleep deprivation. We can force ourselves to perform well when called on, but often we're able to just perform on autopilot.

But autopilot can have bad consequences. The Exxon Valdez oil spill disaster has been attributed, not to rare, bizarre circumstances, but to fatigue of the pilot, who had been working at least 18 hours before the ship ran aground. You don't have to be driving a large oil tanker to be affected. The National Transportation Safety Board attributes about 30% of all fatal accidents on the country's freeways to driver fatigue.

Sleeping less than eight hours a day can also contribute to long-term health consequences. Lack of sleep and sleep deprivation is a stressor to the body's organ systems, including the heart and metabolism. Your body's ability to regulate blood glucose levels is sharply decreased by sleep deprivation. The less sleep you have, the higher your blood glucose, which could result in increased insulin, insulin resistance, increased fat deposition, and diabetes. Increased fat deposition from sleep deprivation is due to increased ghrelin, the appetite hormone, and decreased leptin, the appetite-suppressor hormone.

That's what happens when we don't get eight hours of sleep. So why do we need eight hours?

Good question. There are currently two hypotheses, both of which place the sleep requirement squarely in the brain. There's no information to suggest that the body needs sleep. It's the brain that needs sleep. The two hypotheses are called the neuron adenosine hypothesis and the synaptic hypothesis. Let's take a look at each.

The adenosine hypothesis centers on how neuron brain cells use energy. A group of nerves or neurons near the frontal part of the brain use a substance called adenosine as their energy source and are highly active during the day.

As the neurons fire to send signals among themselves, they leave adenosine behind. This chemical builds up in the space between the neurons, but some of it returns to the neurons and binds to a specialized receptor on the surface of the neurons. This is where sleep is needed

– the more adenosine that binds to the receptors, the less the neurons can fire. Eventually, the surface of the neurons will become completely covered with adenosine stopping the functioning of the neurons and your clear thinking.

This is where the eight hours comes in. It takes eight hours to clear the adenosine and restore balance.

To make this easier to understand, let's look at why caffeine keeps people awake. Caffeine is an anti-adenosine chemical. Caffeine stops the adenosine from binding to the neuron surface specialized receptors. But this is only temporary; no matter how much coffee or other energy drinks you consume, eventually you must sleep to restore the adenosine balance and recharge the brain. We've all experienced the feeling of being both wide awake and exhausted at the same time. That's the brain telling you it needs to restore balance.

The alternate hypothesis, the synaptic hypothesis, is related to nerve connections or synapses that are formed in the brain for learning and memory. We learn and remember because of the way our synaptic connections form. Learning and memory require our neurons to make new connections, form new synapses, and strengthen ones we already have. While we're awake, our brain is actively building an increasing number of synaptic connections from the experiences and events that occur throughout the day.

All that nerve connection building requires space. Neurons are physical entities and therefore have a size, and there are only so many synapses that each neuron can accommodate. And these nerve connecting processes require energy. The neurons reach a point where they have no more energy or space "at the inn." That's the feeling students have while trying to cram for a test when they "hit the wall" and cannot stuff any more information into their heads.

The solution to these space and energy issues is to prioritize synaptic connections. The brain does this by keeping the ones that are needed for new memories or learning a new skill, and refusing space and energy to the ones that no longer matter as much. It's very much like pruning a tree.

That's where the eight hours of sleep comes in. This much time is required for the brain to stop registering new experiences and go "offline." During sleep, the brain can prioritize synapses, decide which ones to keep, how they should be integrated with other ones, and which ones to prune back. How the brain makes these decisions is not known.

However, it appears that synapses increase at an astounding rate during wakefulness and decrease during the night, suggesting evidence for this hypothesis. Also, brainwaves change several times during sleep, but during deepest sleep, the slow delta brainwaves dominate. These waves occur most in areas of the brain concerned with learning, which may indicate the brain is engaged in active pruning.

Whichever hypothesis is correct, and it may be that both or even other processes are also at work, the bottom line is that the brain needs time disengaged from the world's stimulation, and the optimal amount of time, the amount needed to have a Level-10 Energy Day, is about eight hours.

So what are some tried-and-true steps for getting the sleep you need?

Since caffeine stimulates the brain and keeps it going when it wants to come back to balance, limit your caffeine intake late in the day. Get plenty of exercise. Eat well. Avoid alcohol before bedtime. Reduce noise and other distractions such as temperature fluctuations as best as you can. Try not to bring whatever's worrying you to bed; use your mind to clear recurring negative thoughts.

One of the biggest mistakes people make is falling asleep for 30 minutes to an hour while watching TV at 8 or 9 o'clock at night. A midday 20-25 minute nap can be beneficial, but the evening TV nap is deadly; you find yourself tossing and turning all night.

But you can change the habit. First, a little background: bright lights help us set our circadian clock, our bodies' daily rhythms. Therefore it's helpful to limit exposure to bright lights before going to bed. It's also helpful going to bed at the same time each night, add eight hours, and then get out of bed. Not less and not more than eight hours. Doing this keeps your circadian clock in rhythm with the body's natural balance.

Keep in mind that assigning labels can be hazardous. They can set you up for trouble. For example, "I'm not a morning person," or "Don't talk to me in the morning" are myth statements. They set up a neurolinguistic conditioning cycle that, with belief and practice, becomes true. But consider the possibility that there is no such thing as a "morning person."

Regardless, the solution to the sleep-deprivation struggle is simple. Going to bed at the same time each night, adding eight hours, and getting up at the same time each morning will provide the energy needed for a successful day.

There are several ways to help you fall asleep once in bed. Read something that's non-demanding for a few minutes. Or try the countdown method: begin at 100 and slowly count backward to 80. You'll usually fall asleep before reaching that number. Another option is to use self-hypnotic muscle relaxation: begin with your toes, relaxing each one of them; then proceed to your feet, ankles, calves, and knees; moving through the abdomen, chest, arms, neck, and finally the head, deeply relaxing each area of your body. Use your breathing to make this more effective – silently breathe in and out equally without making a sound and remembering to move your lower abdomen up with each in-breath.

If these sleep-inducing methods don't work, and you're still experiencing disrupted or fragmented sleep, then there's a possibility that an actual health condition such as sleep apnea, restless leg movements, hormonal fluctuations, or pain could be responsible for your situation. Some sleeping problems do require a visit to the doctor. Talk to your doctor about these issues, especially if you're experiencing insomnia and cannot get to sleep at all.

But above all, give yourself the time in bed. Some people sleep right through the night. Others sleep in a couple of chunks, waking up for a while before falling asleep again. Others nap for 25 minutes or so in the mid-afternoon. All of these are normal patterns. What matters is that you find what works best for you so that you feel "charged up" for the next day.

---

How's our friend Mark doing? After the challenge with his presentation at work, he made the effort to learn about sleep and applied what he learned.

"Figured out your project?" Jeff asked.

"Yup. Instead of going home and plugging away all night, I got those eight hours of sleep you talked about. Then all the project details just seemed to appear and fell into place. And last night, too, instead of falling asleep watching TV, I stayed awake and read a financial magazine in bed and fell sound asleep after a few minutes."

"Sounds great," Jeff said. "It sounds like that sleep gave you the energy you needed, and may have given you an added bonus of improved confidence."

---

Eight hours of naturally occurring sleep are needed to restore the high-energy brain-cell balance necessary for a successful day. Stimulants and artificial means of interfering with this natural brain restoration will only serve to change an exciting, high-energy day to a weak, low-energy one.

---

Let's find out more about Dave and Kate. After completing his annual physical examination, Dave asked Dr. Anderson some questions.

"I can't sleep. Could you give me some sleeping pills?" Dave pleaded.

"Tell me about your sleep pattern."

"What do you mean?"

"What time do you go to sleep at night? When do you wake up? Do you fall asleep during the day or evening?" Dr. Anderson asked.

"I never thought about it. Every day is different."

"This may be the problem."

"Why? What difference does it make?" Dave asked.

"The brain needs a natural sleep pattern," Dr. Anderson explained. "It requires the same pattern every day to restore the energy chemical balance."

"Oh, I never heard of that," Dave said. "I can tell you about yesterday. It was a typical Wednesday: I came home from work, had a great dinner with Kate, and we watched a TV show we both liked. We had some peanuts and a beer during the show. We didn't bother to change the channel afterward and fell asleep about nine and woke up an hour later."

"Anything else?"

"I was still hungry so I snacked on something from the refrigerator, and we went to bed after midnight. My eyes were wide open and I couldn't sleep. That's why I need your help."

"When did you need to get up for work?"

"I had an early-morning meeting, so the alarm went off a few minutes before six."

"Sounds like five or six hours of sleep," Dr. Anderson said. "You need eight, and that late one hour of snoozing in front of the TV was more disruptive than beneficial. It was way too close to bedtime. The snack you had at midnight also kept you awake."

"I didn't think about the situation." Dave said. "These things just became a habit."

"That's common," the doctor said. "You don't need sleeping pills. You need a good, consistent sleep pattern."

"Sounds boring," Dave said. But feeling curious and desperate, he asked, "How do I do it?"

"Go to bed at the same time every night, add eight hours, and get up."

"That's sounds like a good start," Dave said. "I won't fall asleep during the hours before going to bed."

"Right. Is there anything else you can think of doing or not doing that might help with your sleep pattern?" the doctor asked.

"How about not eating or drinking anything three hours before I go to sleep?" Dave asked.

"That's the answer," Dr. Anderson said. "It'll take you awhile, but stick with it most nights, and it'll pay huge rewards."

The three rules were simple, and though it did take some time, Dave and Kate both developed healthy sleep patterns and noticed a huge improvement in their energy level. They quickly forgot about their TV snoozes and the midnight snacks. The trick was taping their favorite TV shows so they could watch them early in the evening.

# 3

# Exercise Your Way to Energy

**Here's a huge myth:** exercise makes you tired. In fact, it's actually the opposite. Exercise gives you energy. The more exercise you do up to one hour, the more energy you'll have. Exercise gives you a Level-10 Energy Day.

Exercise of just about any type can be beneficial. Try all of them and mix them up. You can exercise in the morning, after work, or whenever you please. You can exercise at a workout facility, a gym, a community center, or at home. You can do it alone or with a group.

It's important to remember that regardless of the exercise, it needs to be performed regularly, and correct form is fundamental. Let's explore how exercise can provide you with unlimited energy.

Exercise increases energy across almost all population groups, and improves mood and energy, even in the absence of fitness improvements. This means that for the most sedentary people, a short bout of 20 minutes of easy exercise can be effective. This includes a brisk walk, swimming, or yoga.

What about fatigue? Did you know that one-quarter of the population reports persistent fatigue? For sedentary people with a low fitness level, the good news is that all it takes is some low-intensity exercise for improvement of fatigue symptoms, such as a 20-minute walk every day. This is an effective way to decrease fatigue for sedentary people, helping them to feel better and become more active. The reason is this: the body and mind respond favorably to simple movement.

So, how does exercise improve energy? The body responds immediately when a person starts exercising. The heart and lungs begin to work, bringing more oxygen and nutrients to cells and carrying away toxins. The powerhouse mitochondria, which are the energy-producing centers of the cells, go into accelerated action. The body's core temperature warms up, increasing chemical reactions. Blood flow increases to the working muscles, improving the transfer of oxygen and nutrients.

Mental clarity improves as the brain responds by increasing the energy and feel-good neurotransmitters norepinephrine, dopamine, and serotonin. Exercise is a natural way to generate these neurotransmitters, which are the same chemicals used as many antidepressant drugs. Strenuous long-duration exercise such as running, swimming, biking, and even yoga will produce endorphins, which reduce pain threshold, decrease stress, and produce a feeling of well-being.

The one-time occurrence of exercise provides increased energy as an acute response, while daily exercise provides the benefits of persistent energy and improved fitness as a chronic response.

Increasing your fitness level through exercise means the body becomes more efficient, basal metabolism is increased, muscles become stronger, and exercise becomes easier. The most exciting improvement that accompanies increased fitness is having more energy, being creative, and enjoying the day. The mind is alive and focused, and physical tasks don't drain energy reserves.

Among people with type-2 diabetes, exercise can improve insulin sensitivity, which allows for better management of blood sugar, leading to fewer diabetic complications. Daily exercise results in both an improved sleeping pattern and daily energy level.

Traditionally, it has been considered that brain cell growth cannot occur in adults, but this has been shown to be wrong as neurogenesis, new brain cell growth, actually can occur in parts of the adult brain. Exercise can result in neurogenesis in the hippocampus, which is the brain's memory center and navigational center. There is a chemical in the brain called brain-derived neurotrophic factor (BDNF) that is used for neurogenesis as a growth factor for these new brain cells. Exercise can increase this growth factor, and the more intense the exercise, the more the neurotrophic factor is increased, up to a certain level. Therefore, exercise has the ability to improve memory.

So what type of exercise is helpful for creating energy? This depends on whether someone is sedentary or exercises on a regular basis. Walking is probably the best exercise for a sedentary person; it can be something as simple and enjoyable as a 20-minute walk around a neighborhood or a walk in a park. The goal is increased energy for the day. If an increased fitness level becomes a goal, this can be accomplished through gradual progression. Avoid too much too soon: jumping into an exercise program that is too intense or complex can cause frustration, injury, and exhaustion. Instead, go slow, and know that the body will improve with each session. Duration, complexity, and intensity can be increased over time.

Begin with the goal of increasing energy for today, each day, and then progress to a healthy goal of at least 150 minutes per week of moderate-intensity aerobic exercise. That's 30 minutes five days a week. Maintaining lean muscle mass is essential for healthy muscles needed for posture, lifting, and climbing. It's also important to combine muscle strengthening exercises at least twice per week to prevent loss of lean muscle mass due to aging.

What time is best for exercising? For a Level-10 Energy Day, morning is best for stimulating the production of energy. Twenty minutes is minimal. In terms of gaining energy, diminishing returns will occur after one hour of strenuous exercise. Exercising at any time is good, but different times of day each have their advantages.

Exercising in the morning provides optimal consistency because it can be incorporated into the morning routine. It raises metabolism, creates energy for the day, and improves mental alertness. In addition, the default waking mental state after a night's sleep is often negative, which can be carried throughout the day, exercising in the morning will disrupt this type of thinking and provide a positive base.

A person exercising at lunch time has the advantage of having a higher body temperature and hormone levels at mid-day. This can regulate lunchtime calorie intake, and provides energy for the afternoon as well as relieving stress. An afternoon workout might be best for improving performance and building muscle due to an increase in hormones.

A nighttime workout relieves stress and limits snacking after dinner.

As exercise becomes more complex, form is fundamental. It's even important for a walk or hike as hunched-over shoulders and shuffling along creates muscle memory that can result in neck pain, low back pain, and misaligned muscle structures. Walking tall with a straight back builds muscles in optimal alignment.

Posture is paramount. In our society, people simply sit too much at a desk, working on a computer, or watching television. Almost always, this posture is with the back stretched out and the chin down or head slumped, positions that have devastating results on the musculoskeletal system.

This is where a personal trainer can be extremely helpful. Certified trainers are educated in proper form and postural deviations. Improved posture results in increased energy because poor posture makes many movements inefficient and painful. Poor posture can cause joints to move improperly. When joints don't function properly, life becomes exhausting and exercise becomes daunting. However, many exercises performed correctly will improve posture, and healthy posture produces energy.

Children and young adults in our society have grown up with video games and computers, and even young athletes now have postural deviations consistent with an older population. Doctors and dentists develop the hunched back and sore neck syndrome as they lean over patients, the operating table, or dental chair throughout the day.

Form is extremely important for muscle-strengthening exercises as specific exercises are designed to develop specific muscle groups. If not learned and done properly, a misaligned exercise can result in muscle pulls and ligament injuries. It's therefore important to learn proper movement patterns and rhythms. Proper form can be used to fix problems, prevent new problems, and ensure maximum benefit from the exercise.

Where should you exercise? Among others, three of the most common options are at home, outdoors, or in a commercial facility. Working out at home is easy but has the disadvantage of being alone, which misses out on the socialization and safety aspects.

Exercise outside is phenomenal when the weather is good, the allergy index is low, and the air quality is high. Exercising in nature has been shown to result in twice as much improvement in mood as exercising indoors. Outdoor exercising results in greater decreases in tension, confusion, anger, and depression. Even five minutes of exercise in green space can improve mood and self-esteem.

For example, some of the top places to run include along the Charles River in Boston, in Central Park in New York City, and along the Salzach River in Salzburg, Austria. The people are interesting, the air is clean, there is always something to look at on a seasonal basis, and the scenery is spectacular. Taking a yoga class or other exercise class on the beach is wonderful; try it during your next coastal visit or vacation. Breaking a sweat outside is a good thing, it keeps you alert; that's how our ancient ancestors survived every day.

Working out at a commercial facility has huge advantages. You can make it convenient and a routine because there are so many locations. The main advantage of working out at a facility is the social aspect of having friends at the facility, and the huge variety of exercise options from free-weights and machines to yoga and spinning classes.

Should you work out alone, with a partner, or a group? This is based on personal preference and personality type. Which are you most likely to be consistent and continue with? Each one has advantages.

Some people like to work out alone because they value their solitary time and set personal goals and challenges for each session.

It's great to have a training partner for one or two workouts a week for safety reasons, such as spotting for lifting, and also for encouragement. A synergy develops with a good partner, which helps to push beyond what a person would do alone.

The group setting for many people is energizing. Spinning, boot camps, and aerobics are great for the motivation and camaraderie.

Is walking at work or having a physically demanding job the same as exercising during non-working time? Yes, compared to someone who does nothing. However, exercise during work does show benefits for a person's mood or energy level. The improvements in mood and energy are received when a person exercises on a regular basis "off the clock."

A walk in the morning, outside, with a friend seems to put it all together, resulting in the greatest enjoyment and benefit.

---

It was a beautiful early fall morning in New England when I was doing a New York City training run along the phenomenal Charles River in Boston. My pleasant thoughts were interrupted with an even more pleasant thought as I saw my future wife coming toward me. My legs on their own volition made the famous U-turn to run beside her and I found myself saying hi to Joan. I didn't get maced, so after some small talk, I asked her for a date, and she accepted. Our first date was at the café above TV's famous *Cheers*, and our second date was the "Halloween Bash" road race, joining 1000 costumed runners through the streets of Boston.

Our first anniversary saw us running the original marathon from Marathon, Greece to the Olympic Stadium in Athens. The six-month training for this was magical, especially the 20-mile tune-up runs three

Sundays before the actual marathon. We ran from our Back Bay location to Wellesley and back, except we never seemed to make it all the way back because we would stop for a huge ice cream "mix-in" with all the extras. It was wonderful running together during the tune-up sessions because we drifted into the blissful alpha-brainwave state and the exercise-released endorphins gave us an extra kick of pleasure.

—

A benefit of exercise? You might meet your spouse.

—

Exercise can relieve stress. I had given a seminar in Kyoto, Japan, about the lung disease I described called bronchiolitis obliterans organizing pneumonia (BOOP). Yes, it's a strange name and maybe a funny name for a lung disease, but the acronym was easy for people to remember. However, my scientist colleagues disagreed. "It's confusing and needs to be eliminated!" they shouted at anyone willing to listen. I was devastated. It was a personal attack on my work. After the meeting I felt angry and stressed, thinking "how could the name be eliminated, it would eliminate all of my efforts?" So I started running along the Kono River, which was located in the center of the city just like the Charles River in Boston, and kept running toward the mountains. One, two, three miles and my mind was still fuming. During miles four and five, I began to calm down. I was near the base of the hills and turned around to run back to the hotel. The issue began to fade in my mind, and it eventually disappeared completely and had no meaning whatsoever. I couldn't have cared less. It became absolutely meaningless and remains so to this day.

—

Exercise is a great stress reliever. A small amount of exercise, like going for a walk outside, is needed for typical stress and more prolonged exercise like running, biking, spinning, Zumba or yoga is needed for big stresses, but if you exercise enough, the stress will most likely be relieved.

—

The morning started slow for Ed and Sue. They drove to their morning workout. For Ed, it was the spin class. For Sue, it was yoga.

As Ed walked in, guys said, "Hey, Ed, great to see you," before he even got on the bike. The spin class began to fill up with the regulars, and there was a barrage of talk, "How's it going," "You're looking good," and "How's the 10K training going?" Throughout the spin class, everyone interacted with the instructor exchanging good-hearted barbs. By the end of the class, Ed was going at high energy. This energy level continued in the locker room with the exchange of upbeat comments with another group of friends. After this socializing, he was fired up and more than ready to start the day.

In another part of the workout facility, Sue had joined her yoga group, and her friend had saved her favorite place for the class. They connected and caught up by talking about their kids. The class began with stretching and challenging body positions, strengthening each muscle group. Sue's friend gave encouragement, which she reciprocated. During the class, the instructor talked about straightening out the mind and dealing with unresolved issues.

Banter among the group of friends continued in the locker room and out the door. Sue's tension had resolved during the session as she gained Level-10 Energy for an exciting day.

—

The social part of exercising with a group and at a commercial workout facility such as a gym or studio is unlike any other situation. It's not like connecting with friends at work. It's not like hanging out with friends at a dinner party or cocktail party or a movie or art opening. It's closest to being with friends at an intense outside sporting event. Why? Because vigorous physical activity such as working out produces those feel-good neurotransmitters including oxytocin, the human bonding hormone neurotransmitter. This bond is created with a special group of wonderful friends who come in all different sizes and shapes, and include moms and dads, doctors, lawyers, bankers, steel workers, carpenters, and mechanics – all having the common bond of sweat and heavy breathing.

Exercise can also give you the feeling of being one year younger for your next birthday. How? There are three types of ages: chronological, biological, and psychological. Chronological age is useful for administrative purposes. Biological age, calculated by age of an organ such as the lungs, and psychological age are meaningful. Your biological age can be 20 to 30 years younger than your chronological age. Exercise and following the Level-10 Energy steps will get you there. For example, my friend, who goes by the name "K", has been following these steps and during a recent spin class, told me, "I'm in better shape now than 30 years ago, and I felt one year younger at my last birthday."

---

A special section is needed for a discussion of a healthy heart, and people who want to push themselves to their maximal capacity. A vigorous, one-hour workout of pushing 200-pound sleds alternating with 20 push-ups and 20 kettle-bell lifts gives a person a great feeling and a tremendous amount of energy. Cyclists in their 40s and 50s can't wait to compete in races and love the feeling of winning – these races take them to sustained heart rates of 160 beats per minute or even higher for hours. They can't stop – they become obsessed with the feeling of competing and winning.

It would be great to work out like this every week and to compete every week, but no matter how much people want to deny reality, the heart muscle and its electrical system change over time, and this becomes a consideration for the senior athlete.

People in their 20s and 30s with healthy hearts can work out and compete with their maximal heart without causing harm. For people in their 40s through 60s and beyond, having a 160 to 170 beats per minute maximal heart rate for too long can cause an abnormal heart rhythm referred to as atrial flutter or atrial fibrillation. This in itself may not be a life-threatening abnormal rhythm, but this aberrant rhythm may not return to normal on its own, or even with medication, so an electrical shock with cardioversion in a hospital setting is needed. Research is underway to further define people at risk and establish a safe heart rate for all ages. In the meantime, keeping a sustained heart rate at a healthy level is a wise decision.

---

Let's check in with Dave and Kate. They're both getting eight hours of sleep a night and have begun to feel an increased energy level.

Leaving her office earlier than usual because of a winter storm, Kate noticed a poster in a shop window announcing that a motivational speaker was giving a seminar about how exercise can change your life.

"Hmm, I'm not much for motivational speakers," she said to herself, "but Dave and I don't exercise, so maybe there's something to exercising that can improve our lives. I think I'll go."

Kate went to the convention hall feeling nervous about seeing someone she knew because it would be embarrassing to admit she needed help. But she quickly found a seat in the back of the room and was soon surprised to discover that she enjoyed what she was learning.

"Dave, we need to start exercising," Kate said excitedly the morning after the seminar. She was motivated! She hadn't told Dave about the seminar because she thought he probably wouldn't have gone, but afterward, she had to tell him.

"What are you saying?" Dave asked, completely uninterested. "The whole world has been telling us to exercise for years, why now? You know I don't like to exercise."

"I have a feeling that it could change our lives. It could give us energy."

"Give us energy? It's exhausting!"

"Not really, but fair enough," Kate said and stopped the discussion for the time being; she didn't want her excitement to be deflated. Instead, she quietly developed a daily exercise program for herself.

Kate had taken some aerobic dance classes in college and remembered enjoying them, so she joined a women's workout facility.

"Welcome, what would you like to do?" Ginny asked.

"Do you have classes?"

"We have about 20 classes during the mornings and evenings," Ginny said enthusiastically. "Which one would you like to take?"

"I'll try the 7:15 step aerobics in the morning."

Kate bought some new workout clothes and arrived early to her first session. She found a step at the back of the class, nervous because she didn't know anyone and didn't want the instructor to criticize her. The instructor flipped on the music from her iPod®, and Kate's nervousness rapidly disappeared. She loved the music and had a great feeling about everyone around her. They were chatting and laughing and seemed to be having a great time.

Kate finished the class and drove to her job with a ton of energy to start the day. She not only had energy, she also felt at peace and felt no stress. She soon made the club a part of her life. She attended several types of classes including yoga, Zumba, a spin class, and a bar and sculpt class. She also had wonderful new friends there who she looked forward to seeing every day.

"Hi Kate," her new friend, Jennifer said, greeting her with a big hug. "I saved a step for you."

"Thanks. How's your daughter doing in soccer?"

"She's doing phenomenal. She has a game tonight."

"Sounds great," Kate said as the music filled the room and they began their routine.

Several months passed and suddenly, Dave developed a frightening illness.

"I can't move," Dave said one morning in a concerned, but non-panicked voice.

"What's going on?" Kate asked with raised eyebrows.

"My shoulders and back are stiff and painful. Even my hips hurt."

They went to the doctor, and after several diagnostic tests, the doctor told Dave, "You have polymyalgia rheumatica."

"What?" Dave asked, confused.

"The condition is called polymyalgia rheumatica. No one knows what causes it," the doctor said. "It's an inflammatory disease like rheumatoid arthritis, but fortunately it's transient and almost always disappears over time. However, we usually need to treat it with the anti-inflammatory steroid medication for several months."

"Sounds complicated," Dave said. "I don't want to take steroids."

"Your concern is understandable," the doctor replied. "This type of steroid is not the muscle-building type; it's the anti-inflammatory type called prednisone."

"I've heard of that," Kate said, "my friend had a bad asthma attack and had to take prednisone. She had a puffy face and gained weight."

"Yes, those are some of the side effects," the doctor said. "We will review them in detail so you can monitor them. Most are reversible, but some can be serious."

"You're right about the reversible part," Kate said, "my friend needed them for a short time. She was completely normal after the prednisone, and after that, she began using a steroid inhaler instead of the pills."

"Dave, I have a tip for you," the doctor said. "You're going to have stiff muscles and pain, and you're not going to feel like doing much, but an exercise program can do wonders for you."

"Exercise? If I'm in pain, isn't exercising the last thing I'll want to do?"

"Maybe, but here's the irony: the polymyalgia will be easier to manage. The exercise will also smooth out the highs and lows of the steroid treatment. Be careful at first, but you should gradually develop a daily exercise program."

"Sounds like I need to do this, but it also sounds like a lot of effort and discipline," Dave said.

"Oh, I know it'll work," Kate said. "Don't worry about the discipline. It becomes so much of a good part of your day, you'll be upset if you can't make it to a workout."

Dave began his exercise program slowly, just a few minutes every other day. He gradually increased his workout to one hour every day. He joined a workout facility located on the way to work. He changed up his exercise routine: sometimes it was the elliptical, sometimes it was light strength training, and he even did a spin class once a week. He stayed at the back of the class so he could go at his own pace, but he found it supportive and a great social hour. With the help of a physical therapist and trainer he did exercises that worked around his muscle pain and stiffness. These exercises gave him a huge amount of energy, and as the doctor had said, they smoothed out the highs and lows of the prednisone treatment. The polymyalgia rheumatica lasted for several months but gradually disappeared.

After resolution of his illness, Dave realized that exercise gave him so much energy that he continued working out every day. He became as enthusiastic as his wife, and they often shared stories about their friends at the club. When they traveled, Dave and Kate worked out together, going to a spin class or an outdoor exercise class on the beach. These sometimes became a vacation highlight.

---

Dave's life changed dramatically after he started exercising. It helped him cope with his medical condition and gave him a tremendous amount of energy. In the next chapter, we'll find out how Dave and Kate learned to eat the right foods for lifelong energy.

# 4

# The "Big Three" Foods for Unlimited Energy:

## Lean Protein, Omega-3's, and Slow-Burn Carbs

**The right foods** will give you phenomenal energy for the entire day. The wrong foods will leave you lacking energy, and some foods will even sap your energy leaving you nonproductive and lethargic.

Overeating is a built-in default for all of us. Because of this, you need to have enough thinking space to ensure that you eat the right foods in the right amounts. You need to be fully aware when choosing what to eat. Think about it, when your mind is filled with stress, deadlines, work, and social activities, you don't think about what you're eating and how much. It's too low of a priority. Your mind is busy thinking about everything else. Unaware, random eating is fraught with hazards. When you're not paying attention, the tendency is to keep eating until you're completely stuffed. Not only will this result in increased fat deposition and artery inflammation, but also a total loss of energy. After all, how do you feel when you're stuffed?

It's important to train your mind so that making the right choices becomes automatic and does not require extra thinking.

What are the energy-producing foods? There are three of them: lean protein, omega-3 polyunsaturated fats, and slow-burn low-glycemic or low blood sugar carbohydrates. Let's take a look at each of these in greater detail.

Lean protein is pure energy, and doesn't cause inflammation or fat deposition. Animal and fish protein are good sources, but it's important to choose these wisely.

Skinless chicken trimmed of fat, boiled in water, and rinsed with water is an excellent source of protein. Initially, the taste can seem bland, but over a two-week period, the taste buds adjust, and the subtle flavor of boiled chicken becomes real. This can be improved quickly with sodium-free herbs and spices and slow-burn, low-glycemic vegetables.

Fish such as salmon and cod are excellent sources of pure protein and have the extra advantage of containing omega-3 fatty acids, the protective anti-inflammatory fatty acids.

Is mercury in fish a problem? It could be, but mostly it's not. Mercury is a common element in the Earth's surface, and as fuel is burned around the world, mercury can become airborne, settling in rivers, lakes, and oceans. Fish and aquatic plants such as plankton and algae ingest mercury as part of their feeding cycle. In addition, larger fish absorb mercury as they eat smaller fish. For people, and especially pregnant women, eating large amounts of certain types of fish could result in accumulating high enough mercury levels to cause the symptoms of mercury poisoning.

The mercury level in fish varies from harmless amounts to large amounts that need to be limited. We determine the amount of mercury we ingest by learning about the levels of mercury in fish. Sensitivity to mercury varies from person to person; however, the amount of mercury will disappear over time as less mercury is ingested.

Which fish have high mercury levels? The ones with big mouths that live the longest such as shark, blue-fin tuna, and swordfish. Low mercury levels are found in salmon, trout, sole, and cod. The latter group can be eaten on a weekly basis; the big fish should be eaten less frequently. Shellfish have low levels of mercury.

Enjoy fish. It's a great source of high-energy protein and anti-inflammatory omega-3 fatty acids.

Vegetable and legume proteins are an excellent source of energy. Their natural pure form is best with no added ingredients. Raw vegetables need to be thoroughly washed to eliminate hazardous bacteria and unwanted chemicals. Steamed vegetables are excellent because the healthy nutrients are not destroyed. Some vegetables such as spinach can be sautéed at low heat with water or olive oil without losing their benefits. Salt does not need to be added to vegetables; there is sufficient sodium in naturally-occurring foods. Healthy spices such as ginger or turmeric in curry powder can be added to vegetables for taste.

High-protein plant foods include legumes such as soybeans, chickpeas, pinto beans, kidney beans, and lentils; and nuts such as almonds. These foods contain up to 20 grams of protein per 100-gram portion. Grains such as whole oats, whole wheat, quinoa, couscous, and barley contain up to 15 grams of protein.

Whey is a remarkable protein. More than 8,000 years ago, it was found that aged milk separates into liquid whey and solid curd. The whey was discarded and the curd was made into cheese. However, 5,600 years ago Hippocrates demonstrated that whey could be used as a quickly absorbed protein for growth and strength. During the 1500s, Swiss pig farmers realized that their pigs grew faster and bigger when they ate whey, so they tried it themselves with dramatic results. In the 1600s and 1700s spas sprang up throughout Europe touting the strength-giving powers of whey. In the early 1900s, a digestible powder form was developed, in the 1960s, the sugary lactose was removed, and in the 1980s, the fat was removed so now pure whey protein is available.

Whey has low naturally-occurring sodium and high potassium levels. It contains all 20 essential amino acids and has one of the highest scores for ease of digestion. It has a high level of lysine amino acid, which is a fundamental growth protein for children, and therefore has been used as a basis for infant formulas. Whey protein also has appetite-suppressant and anti-inflammatory properties, and it's a slow-burn, low-glycemic food that does not increase blood sugar. The hydrolysate form is often used by athletes because of its rapid absorption.

Some people have developed whey protein sensitivity and are not able to consume whey. However, people who have developed casein protein sensitivity, the cheese portion of fermented milk, or those who have developed lactose intolerance, can usually consume the pure whey protein.

What about fats? The right ones can give you a huge amount of energy and prevent inflammation of the arteries, especially the small arteries feeding life to the heart. Which ones are they? They're the unsaturated fatty acids.

Specifically, they're the omega unsaturated fatty acids that include omega-3, omega-6, and omega-9. Additional technical detail is needed here because research has discovered that all of them are beneficial, but a balance is necessary as there are important differences among them. For example, omega-6 may be out of balance. There may be too much omega-6 compared to omega-3. The omega number is used to show the location of the bonding site of the unsaturated fatty acid.

The omega-3 fatty acids circulate in the blood as high-density lipoproteins (LDH) and protect your blood vessels because they have anti-inflammatory properties. Fish oil has two common ones: docosahexaenoic acid or DHA, and eicosapentaenoic acid or EPA. Plant oils from seeds such as flax contain the omega-3 fatty acid, alpha-linolenic acid or ALA. Other foods containing omega-3s include cold-water fish such as salmon, cod, mackerel, trout, and herring as well as walnuts, flaxseed, and green leafy vegetables such as spinach and rapini.

Some omega-6 fatty acids have anti-inflammatory properties while others can become inflammatory. Linoleic acid is the common one found in vegetable cooking oils such as corn oil, canola oil, sunflower oil, and soybean oil. It is also found in nuts and seeds. Linoleic acid is an essential fatty acid; however, too much in relation to omega-3 fatty acids can increase inflammation. The typical American diet may have 15 to 30 times more omega-6s, so it's important to strive for a balance of omega-3s to omega-6s. Too much arachidonic acid can be inflammatory for individuals with an inflammatory disorder, while gamma-linoleic acid (GLA) appears to be an anti-inflammatory omega-6 fatty acid. Processed foods may contain too much of the omega-6 inflammation-type fatty acids and should be limited or eliminated.

Omega-9 fatty acids are found in animal fat and vegetable oils. Olive oil contains oleic acid, a common omega-9 fatty acid, but it's the antioxidant polyphenols in olive oil that provide the major health benefits. Peanut oil contains oleic acid, but also contains the omega-6 arachidonic acid that can cause inflammation in some situations. A rule of thumb is to read the labels and consume the omega-3 fatty acids.

Let's talk about carbohydrates. These foods are available everywhere 24 hours a day and they're cheap – the perfect combination for the consumption of the wrong ones.

For energy, the best approach is to understand the difference between slow-burn and fast-burn carbohydrates as they relate to blood sugar levels and insulin release. Produced by the pancreas, insulin is a powerful, life-sustaining hormone that regulates blood sugar levels. It's fundamental to energy management because too much insulin release turns carbohydrates into fat deposition and inflammatory triglycerides.

Therefore, it's best to focus on the slow-burn carbohydrates. They're the answer to high-energy production because they don't cause a surge in blood sugar. Slow-burn carbs include vegetables such as spinach, rapini, and broccoli, and are in the same league as legumes such as beans and peas. Eating these vegetables and legumes results in pure energy. Fruit such as apples and clementines are energy producers because they contain fructose, the sweet-tasting sugar metabolized in the liver. Fructose in moderation does not cause a blood sugar surge.

Fiber is also a great slow-burn carbohydrate for energy generation because fiber keeps the system flowing and binds with toxic substances to eliminate them. Importantly, fiber in foods can prevent peaks of blood sugar levels. Insoluble fiber is the woody portion of plant-based foods, such as broccoli and asparagus stems, and can regulate bowel function and keep things moving. Soluble fiber is the gummy substance in oatmeal and red beans. The beta-glucan in soluble fiber can decrease the blood level of low-density lipoprotein or LDL, which is a fatty transport protein in the blood that at high levels causes inflammation and thickening of the arteries.

You know about the fast-burn carbs – they're the sugary foods such as pastries, cakes, pies, candy, and sugary drinks. But there are other fast-burn carbs that may not immediately come to mind. They are the white starchy foods such as white potatoes, white rice, pasta, and breads. Minimize these high-glycemic carbohydrates. The term "glycemic index" is useful because it indicates how high the blood sugar goes after eating a particular food. It's also related to the amount of food intake, so it's possible to eat a small quantity of high-glycemic food without causing a surge in blood sugar.

The problem is that these sugary foods and French fries or chips are almost impossible to eat in a small enough amount to prevent triggering the insulin response. Try eating one French fry, one chip, or one sip of a smoothie. The insulin release is going to trigger two events: cortisol release causing fat deposition and high blood triglycerides causing inflamed arteries. Both of these responses are major energy destroyers.

High-energy foods are high-quality foods. They're simple, nonprocessed foods. They're grown as naturally as possible with personal attention. They're fruits and vegetables grown organically from well-cultivated fields without pesticides. They're from free-range chickens and cattle. They're free-swimming fish in rivers, lakes, and oceans. They're nonprocessed carbohydrates that have not been fructose-condensed by a manufacturing process, and oils that have not been hydrogenated. Too much high-fructose corn syrup and hydrogenated fat in oils will cause increased triglycerides and inflammation of the arteries. Whether shopping or eating, seek out high-quality foods.

---

Joe loved food. Unfortunately, he also loved all the wrong types of food. His protein came from fat-laden steaks, hamburgers, hot dogs, sausages, deep-fried chicken, and seafood fried in tasty batter. He ate his saturated fats and fast-burn carbohydrates from these fried foods, in addition to French fries, chips, pastries, candy bars, and ice-cream smoothies.

It seemed everything Joe ate was among the three groups of fat-laden protein, saturated fats, and fast-burn carbs. For breakfast he had fried eggs, breakfast potatoes, bacon, and white toast with jelly. He had a couple of muffins for a morning snack. For lunch, he had hamburgers, French fries, and an ice-cream shake. He had potato chips and pastry treats for his afternoon snack at work. For dinner, he had fried calamari, chicken parmesan, spaghetti with meatballs, and pie with ice cream. Later, he had a hot dog and popcorn while watching TV before going to bed.

With this diet, Joe had an energy level-5 most of the day, and often it decreased to level-3 while at other times it bounced to level-8 for a few minutes after eating sugary foods. His energy level was bad enough, but as you might imagine, he was dangerously overweight, and he had diabetes and hypertension. The fast-burn carbohydrates produced the excess weight, and the saturated fats and triglycerides from those fast-burn carbs produced arteries filled with plaques that could cause a heart attack at any time.

Susan also loved food, but her preferences were different. She had a grapefruit and eggs mixed with spinach and tomatoes for breakfast. Her lunch was a small portion of boiled, lean skinless chicken with a lemon-artichoke sauce. She ate unsalted walnuts for a snack. In the evening she had salmon seasoned with turmeric, rapini, lentils, and a small amount of tomatoes and avocado on the side. She used three important taste sensations including foods that had a bitter taste from green vegetables, an astringent taste from legumes, and a pungent taste from herbs. These foods gave Susan a Level-10 Day, plus she was healthy with no diabetes, no hypertension, and no heart disease.

Who are you, Joe or Susan? If you're Joe, how can you stop eating these foods? First, learn about the good ones and second, train your brain to choose foods that are safe and will give you high energy. Choose slow-burn carbohydrates, unsaturated fats, and lean protein. Over time, it will become a habit, and the "healthy and safe" taste of these high-energy foods will replace the sweet, salty, and sugary taste of low-energy foods.

Use positive feedback to train your brain. Each time you eat these three foods, enjoy the long-lasting positive feeling you experience. This feeling is so much better than the short-lasting, fleeting feeling from the high-glycemic sugary foods that leave you out of energy and craving for more.

---

What is the right amount of these foods? Let me introduce an idea called eating to your high-energy level. For centuries, monks and seers have known that food brings energy up to a certain point when the energy peaks, levels off, and then falls. These ancients learned how to determine when they'd reached the highest level, and then stop. It's a subtle internal signal and takes time to learn because the natural stimulus toward achieving the filled-up feeling is related to the stomach stretch receptor signal, which is much too slow. Once a person reaches the filled-up feeling, it's too late; the energy peaked much earlier and by then the energy has been lost. Use the ancients as role models. Learn to eat to your high-energy level, not to your over-full, stuffed level.

Train your brain for the feeling of eating to your high-energy level. What is the feeling? It varies from person to person. I experience a pleasant, calming effect. Some people can feel the increase in their blood sugar. Someone said she began to sneeze. Whatever the feeling may be for you, learn it. The feeling of your high-energy level can save your life.

Foods with anti-inflammatory properties are energy producers. These are the flavonoids that are the color in foods. They make up a group of naturally-occurring compounds found in colorful yellow, red, and purple fruits, and vegetables such as spinach, eggplant, and kidney beans. Red, orange, and yellow peppers are good choices. They can keep your blood vessels flexible by inhibiting synthesis of the low-density fatty lipoproteins that cause inflammation. Citrin can, too. It's the most active flavonoid in the citrus fruit lemon.

Herbs and spices can also be a source of energy. Some, such as ginger and turmeric in curry powder, may have anti-inflammatory action and prevent arterial plaque formation. Rosemary can act as an antioxidant and prevent formation of toxic compounds produced in grilled, broiled, or fried foods.

Along with making the optimal high-energy food choices, it is also important to be aware of your eating patterns. Do not let eating be an unconscious habit. Eat sitting down. Do not do anything else while eating, such as riding up an elevator or standing in line. Eat when your stomach is empty, usually every three to four hours. Eat when the food in your mouth has been swallowed. The tongue has taste buds for six flavors. It's helpful to stimulate all six taste centers for improved digestion and energy. Eat meals with the six tastes of sweet, sour, salt, bitter from leafy green vegetables, pungent from legumes, and astringent from spices.

Resisting food cravings can result in positive feelings and energy. How can you manage temptation and cravings? Often, as the day progresses, our mental energy is too depleted to fight temptation. This may be depletion of a neurotransmitter such as phenylethylamine or PEA, which is synthesized in the brain from the amino acid phenylalanine.

Making low-energy poor food choices is a conditioned response. But there is hope. You can train your brain to become unconditioned by listening to your body. Listen to your belly brain. It's called the enteric nervous system – the separate but interconnected nervous system that works along your entire intestinal tract. There are as many neurons in your enteric nervous system as in your spinal cord, which gives the system the ability to exchange valuable information to make high-energy healthy food choices.

Teaming up with your body will enable you to produce the highest level of energy. If you crave a poor food choice, try this unconditioning response by eating the food, then notice the feeling of your body rejecting it. As soon as this happens, feel the positive effect of not eating the low-energy, poor quality food. Eventually the body will reject memories connected with poor food choices and instead will replace them with the new pleasure of the body's positive response to eating healthy foods.

---

Let's update Dave and Kate's story to find out how they're doing with modifying their eating habits. Will they eat foods that give them energy for the day, or will they opt for the fast-carb burners that leave them drained? Soon after they developed an excellent sleep pattern and were exercising regularly, Dave and Kate learned of the bad effects of fast-burn carbohydrates and saturated fats.

"I found out about the two most dangerous foods on the planet today," Dave told Kate during a trip to the grocery store.

"You're scaring me," Kate said nervously.

"I'm being a little dramatic, but you know what they are and why they're dangerous."

"I do?" Kate asked.

"They're the fast-burning sugary carbohydrates and the saturated fats," Dave said. "They cause belly fat, diabetes, clogged arteries, and heart attacks."

"But, I've heard that saturated fats are healthy."

"In small amounts, fatty acids like stearic acid and palmitic acid actually are healthy," Dave said, "but the safe amount is so small, it's laughable. Try eating one French fry or one potato chip."

"So why are these unhealthy foods so readily available? They're everywhere!"

"No easy answer to that question," Dave said. "Years of conditioning and eating habits probably. Not to mention marketing and advertising. Cheap, mass-produced processed foods are part of our culture. You know, all that marketing could be just as effective for advertising healthy foods."

"So, what do we do about it?"

"Take the grassroots approach. One person at a time. Make healthy choices."

"So what are the healthy choices?" Kate asked.

"I've heard that three food categories will produce real energy," Dave said. "So keep it simple: lean protein, unsaturated fats, and slow-burn carbs."

"So lean protein means salmon, skinless chicken, and plant protein, right?" said Kate.

"Yes, and unsaturated fats include a balance of the different omega acids especially from fish and plants," Dave said.

"So which carbs are slow-burn?" Kate asked.

"Well, they're the ones that are slowly metabolized without increasing the blood sugar level, like green vegetables, colorful fruit, and fiber."

"Sounds good. But you know that once you choose these good foods you have to then prepare them in healthy ways," Kate said.

"What do you mean?" Dave asked.

"You have to prepare the foods correctly," Kate answered. "Melissa was telling me all about it at workout. Steamed vegetables and fish are excellent. We should limit fried foods."

"How do you steam vegetables?" Dave asked.

"I guess it's easy. You just put a little water in the bottom of a sauce pan, add vegetables, place tinfoil on top of the broccoli, and put the lid on the pan. You heat at low to medium temperature, enough to produce steam without boiling away the water. Like ten minutes or so. And add no salt."

"But," she continued, that's not enough. It's also critical to be aware of the amount of food you're eating so you don't eat too much. That's probably the number one problem, eating too much," Kate emphasized.

"Easy to say, impossible to do," Dave said with a sigh.

"That's why we need to learn how to eat at our high-energy level," Kate said.

"Now you've lost me," Dave said. "What are you talking about?"

"I learned about this during yoga class. As you eat, the food provides energy, but over time, the energy peaks and falls off, and then completely plummets if you become holiday-stuffed."

"Yeah, that stuffed feeling is distressing," Dave said.

"We have to listen to our bodies in order to learn the feeling of peak energy, and then stop eating once we reach it," Kate said.

"So how do you learn? Dave asked.

"The feeling is subtle. Melissa told me that you have to pay attention to learn it, but if you think about it, you know. Some people have a feeling that their blood sugar is starting to increase and others have a feeling in their mind. Once you learn it, it becomes much easier to recognize, and can become an unconscious sensing."

"So, how do you stop?"

"Melissa told me that at first, it takes concentration and brain power," Kate said. "You need to force yourself to stop. After enough times, it becomes a habit and automatic."

"It would be great to learn to stop eating at the peak energy level," Dave replied.

"Let's do it," Kate said.

---

It took some time, but Dave and Kate were amazed by how eating lean protein, the omega fatty acids, and slow-burn carbs in the right amount dramatically increased their energy.

5

# Learning is Energy on Wheels

**Not many people like to study,** and even fewer like to take tests, but everyone likes to learn. New and constant learning can activate and increase energy. Learn something new every day. Just keep learning.

Learn by reading books. Learn by searching the internet and watching web videos like the TED talks about "ideas worth spreading." You can buy educational CDs. You can listen to an entire university course while driving or doing low-level work.

The benefits of learning something new are continually being revealed through research. People who constantly learn have improved self-reported health indices, and they have reduced risk of depression. Other benefits include improved well-being and increased self-confidence. Learning engages the brain and creates new neuronetworks. Learning slows the decline of reasoning and memory, and decreases the risk of developing dementia or Alzheimer's disease.

Learning random topics not related to your work or your routine activities can ignite the imagination and provide energy. For example, the next several paragraphs are related to arbitrary topics that I have explored.

You can learn how humans learn. Learning occurs from repeated synaptic responses creating pathways in the hippocampus region of the brain. The process occurs through the glutamate neurotransmitter that stimulates long-term potentiation pathways. A second, more powerful two-receptor system has been discovered. This means if enough glutamate is stimulated, it opens a second receptor that floods the receptor with calcium causing a huge spark of energy resulting in the pronouncement of "Now I get it!"

There are scores of other subjects you can learn about. For example, you can learn to "think like an economist." These are some of the things you'll learn. People respond to incentives, both positive and negative. Want to discourage people's actions? Add a tax. Want to encourage people's actions? Make the action tax deductible. Pay attention to "opportunity costs" in addition to actual money costs. Consider time lost, gasoline cost, wear and tear cost, when driving 20 miles for a $5.00 savings. When there's change, whether at our work, economic change, or in our society; it's not a single change. It's always complex and many changes are taking place. Watch for unanticipated influences and unintended consequences. Pay attention to the margins or fringes of any activity.

You can learn about quantum physics and bosons. During the 1920s, physics Professor Satyendra Bose was lecturing to his students about basic physics, and he asked them if they had object A and object B and two buckets, how many combinations of object A and B could be placed in each bucket? That's easy, it's four, the students answered quickly: AA, AB, BA, and BB.

"It's three!" exclaimed Professor Bose. The students thought he was incompetent and the published lecture brought ridicule from other physicists, but not from Albert Einstein. He realized it was one of the most important discoveries of the century, and it became a fundamental part of quantum physics. Why? The students and other physicists assumed object A and object B were two different objects resulting in four combinations; however, if object A and object B were identical, there would be three. Even with this explanation, skepticism remained because physics was founded on the snowflake and sand particle theories – no two snowflakes and no two particles of sand are identical. That is true; however, for quantum physics, Bose and Einstein told the world there are subatomic energy particles in the universe that are identical. They're called bosons after Bose and Einstein.

Almost a century later, these bosons have been well-studied and solved another enigma. What's light? It acts like a particle, and it acts like a wave, but which is it? Light consists of photons which are energy particle bosons able to act as both particles and waves. Helium atoms are another example of bosons. They're identical and group together; at near absolute-zero temperature, they have the strange behavior of flowing up and down a glass container. As bosons attract each other, there is an opposite energy particle called fermions, which repel each other, and stabilize the universe.

Genetics has become a major field of study. For example, epigenetics has emerged as a study of the effects of the environment on DNA. The health of the mother and father is reflected in the offspring, which can be carried through several future generations. Pregnancy during a period of starvation will result in illnesses and shorter life expectancy for the offspring from too much methylation of the DNA. Methylation means that one carbon atom and three hydrogen atoms form a methyl molecule, which can become attached to DNA disrupting the in-born DNA instructions for healthy cell growth, resulting in unhealthy cell reactions such as inflammation.

Epigenetics has shown that babies born of a mother after the mother has gastric bypass surgery have a healthier weight than babies born before the surgery. Another example comes from a study of three generations in Sweden beginning from the 1890s comparing amount of food available and health of offspring. It was found that if food was scarce for the father just before puberty, offspring were less likely to die from heart disease. But if food was too plentiful for the paternal grandfather during the time period just before puberty, death related to diabetes was increased in the grandchildren. These examples show that certain types of environmental factors can directly change the DNA.

You can learn about neurotransmitters. Messages in the brain are transmitted across two brain cell neurons by chemicals called neurotransmitters, which are stored in packets at the end of the neuron and change a chemical signal into an electrical signal by a corresponding receptor like a lock and key. Some excite the neuron and others inhibit the neuron. There are more than 100 neurotransmitters in the brain and more in other parts of the body.

Too little or too much of a specific neurotransmitter can cause problems. For example, Parkinson's disease occurs from an insufficient amount of dopamine in a specific region of the brain, while schizophrenia results from too much dopamine. So treating Parkinson's with dopamine is effective, but all of the brain receives the extra dopamine, not only the Parkinson's region, so the side effects are schizophrenia-type symptoms. The opposite occurs when treating schizophrenia with anti-dopamine medications.

You can learn about money. Although not equally distributed, money is abundant. Making money does not mean taking it away from someone else; an unlimited amount is available to everyone. It's not a game of win or lose. Money can be made without depriving others. Some people are taught as children that there are two types of people: those with good jobs that improve other's lives through service, and those who are rich. It's either one or the other; you can't be both. And being rich is bad. This limiting belief has frustrated talented and dedicated people from accomplishing potentially highly beneficial goals to society. People who are rich can have unlimited compassion and a huge heart to match their bank accounts. Having money to do something good for people or improve people's lives is a good thing, and having more money lets even more good things happen.

"Money is the root of all evil" is a saying that has been shortened over time from the original, which was that "the 'love of' money is the root of all evil." However, money itself is neutral. It's not good or bad. It's a form of energy. It's what people do with money that creates harm or benefit.

Learn about other random topics. Read or hear about successful people. For example, learn that John Mackey, the founder of Whole Foods Market, has developed his perspective of American capitalism, which includes providing motivation for people to want to work for a company. In the past, it's been taught the purpose of a company is to maximize profits for shareholders. Not so for John Mackey, who is of the opinion that people don't want to work to increase the wealth of shareholders. His view is that the reason for a company is to have a purpose, and that people want to know that the work they're doing is contributing to helping others and making the world a better place. He feels that a company needs social responsibility including fair trade, environmental stewardship, and supporting local businesses.

People can learn a better way of doing something, even after 25 to 50 years of doing something the same way? For example, how do you park your car in a parking lot when there are several lines of parking spaces available? Do you pull into the front lane of two-lane parking spots so that when you return, you back out? There's an easier and safer way. If available, drive past the first parking spot into the spot where your car is pointing outward. When you return, simply drive forward out of that parking spot. Then you won't have to strain your neck by looking around several times to avoid cars, people, and animals, nor will you have to worry about hitting another car or a person because you can't see them, nor will you have to worry about someone backing into you because they didn't see you. Try it. It's easier, safer, healthier, and less stressful.

—

Let's check in on Dave and Kate. They've learned about high-energy foods. Can they now use learning to give them energy?

"Kate, I have to tell you what I learned," Dave said excitedly.

"What's that?"

"It's called remote viewing," Dave said.

"Remote what?"

"It's a way of using the mind with your eyes closed to see, taste, smell, and feel things in the past."

"Sounds crazy," Kate said.

"It's a little strange, but it's interesting, and I enjoyed it," Dave said. "You can actually visualize events with your mind, like an oil-field fire and even smell the burning oil. You can see ancient buildings."

"How does it work?" Kate asked.

"Universal energy is like a hologram. Each particle of a hologram contains the whole image. Quantum physics states that each energy particle in the universe contains the past, present, and future. You just need to tune in."

"Sounds like science fiction," Kate said skeptically. "How do you know it's true?"

"You've had an experience when you were randomly thinking about your college roommate 20 or 30 years later, when suddenly the phone rings, and it's your college roommate. How does this happen? Statistical variation or through universal energy?"

"How did you learn remote viewing?" Kate asked.

"I listened to a course in the car while going to work, and with my earphones for some of the exercises because you can't drive while you're doing them. There's a five-day course that's also offered periodically throughout the year. We should go sometime."

"Hmm, a little too strange for me, but maybe."

"There's no harm, and it's a learning experience without any downside, except being embarrassed because you can't believe you will actually see a remote event with you mind," Dave said.

Kate and Dave attended the next class, and found it was an interesting experience, and the alpha brainwaves needed to perform the activity filled them with energy.

Next, it was Kate's turn to suggest a new learning experience. "Let's take dancing lessons," she said to Dave one evening after work.

"Hold it. I've gone along with all of these things about sleep, exercise and the right foods, but I can't go dancing."

"Why not?"

"I don't want to dance with a stranger."

"We can take private lessons, so it's just you and me."

"OK, sounds good, let's go."

Kate signed them up for a weekly lesson. Dave didn't have to worry about changing partners and dancing with strangers.

"That was great," Dave said after the fifth lesson, "and practicing at home was enjoyable. Dancing together produces a lot of energy."

"Yup, it's enjoyable, and I liked flying around the dance floor with you and learning the moves."

---

Learn something new. You'll be amazed at how much energy you can create. You also might learn something that will help someone else. Always keep learning.

# 6

# Brainwaves:
## Using Your Mind to Create Energy

**The body is made up** of a powerful energy system. The universe has an infinite amount of energy that continues to increase every day.

You can experience Level-10 Energy yourself. Here is one way to feel the energy: with your mind, focus your attention on your hand and visualize the healthy, vibrant cells. Then visualize the nucleus of the cells, then the molecules, and then the atoms of these cells. At the level of the atom feel the power of the nucleus and the electrons flying at the speed of light at huge distances, as far from each other as the sun is from the earth. Put yourself at the subatomic level in between the nucleus and the electrons. You are now surrounded by subatomic packets or particles of pure energy. Each particle is identical to the other particle. The particles are gregarious melding together giving you Level-10 Energy. Stay there as long as you wish. Breathe in the energy, feel the energy, and become Level-10 Energy.

Now with your mind, go the other direction as if you're hovering above your current location looking down. Then hover above the earth, then above the solar system, and then far out above the Milky Way. Now visualize yourself half way between the Milky Way and the end of the expanding universe. You are in vast space and surrounded by Level-10 Energy packets of energy. Stay here and feel the immense power of the surrounding Level-10 Energy. You're now in the alpha brainwave state; let your mind feel the energy for creativity, compassion, gratitude, and success.

That's fuel for life. That's Level-10 Energy.

Use your breathing to create energy. The body is made up of cycles of energy. You can use your breathing to join these cycles. Here's the short version of how to do it.

Though this can be a traditional eyes-closed meditation, I prefer eyes open. As you breathe in, use your mind to bring in energy from the bottom of your spine to the top of your head, and as you breathe out, complete the loop by breathing out energy back to the bottom of the spine. Continue breathing in energy from the bottom of the spine to the top of the head and breathing out energy from the top of the head back to the bottom of the spine making a continuous oval loop of energy.

Move your attention to your chest. Using your mind, breathe in energy through an imaginary opening in the center of your chest and breathe out, forming a cycle of energy. Continue to breathe, bringing in more energy with each breath.

Next, focus on the bottom of your feet. Using the mind, bring in energy through an imaginary opening in the bottom of both feet, and bring the energy throughout the body all the way to your head and then back down again, breathing out through your feet.

The last cycle is with your hands. Using your mind, first pay attention to the energy in the palm of your right hand; then move the energy to the palm of your left hand. You can feel the sensation. Repeat this once. Then breathe in energy through the palms of your outstretched hands, making a cycle through your arms and chest and returning the energy to your hands. Breathe in more energy with each breath. Your hands will tingle with the energy.

Since this is a mind exercise, you'll improve with practice. You'll be able to generate an unlimited amount of energy.

As mentioned above, you can do this while sitting in a chair or on a pile of pillows with eyes closed, but you can also practice this with your eyes open, during a walk or hike, which provides the added benefit of exercise. You can also do this during a light run, swimming, cross-country skiing, or just about anything. Just take some time to learn more about the process of focused breathing and energy generation.

Breathe silently in and out, without holding your breath at the top or the bottom of the breath. Breathe equally in and out, and move your lower abdomen out as you inhale.

After you've stabilized your breathing, you need to relax all of your muscles and release all tension in all the muscle groups. Using your mind, focus on an area and relax it. Release the tension. Begin with your eyelids, your eyes, your face, the top and back of the head. Relax your neck. You are slowly breathing in and out while you're relaxing the muscles. Using your mind, move to your shoulders and relax them, now the middle back, the lower back and then your chest. Relax your abdomen with a few belly breaths by breathing in and lifting your abdomen. Return your attention to relaxing your upper arms, lower arms and hands, and finish by relaxing your upper and lower legs and your feet.

As you continue, you're breathing slowly without making a sound. Your muscles are completely relaxed. For your mind to fully circulate energy, you now need to disengage your ongoing self-talk – that continuous stream of thoughts in the frontal brain. One way to do this is to move your attention to the center of the brain between the two hemispheres, behind the tongue. Visualize you're sitting on a pile of soft pillows peering out through the eyes and looking at a distant, nondescript, hazy light. Continue quiet breathing, and now you are completely disengaged from the clattering mind. Repeat the process as the chattering thoughts reappear.

As you breathe in, visualize a circulating energy loop moving from the bottom of your spine up to the top of your head and returning back down the front of the spine to the bottom of the spine. It's a continuous loop of energy, always moving. As you breathe in, move the energy from the bottom to the top of the spine and say the word "strength" to yourself. As you breathe out, send the energy from the top of your head, down the front of the spine and to the end of the spine, and say "grace." It's a balance of energy, breathing in strength and breathing out grace. Continue this for a few minutes, enjoying the feeling of energy.

Now, do the same thing with your chest. As you breathe in, visualize energy coming into your chest and breathing out, sending energy out of the chest, making a continuous loop of energy in and energy out. With each breath, bring in more energy than the previous breath, not by breathing deeper, but by using your mind. With this breathing, say the word "compassion" for yourself with each breath in and compassion for everyone else with each breath out. Continue this for several breaths and feel the energy grow throughout your chest.

Now, do the same thing for your feet. Visualize bringing energy through the bottom of your feet as if there are openings allowing the energy in. Breathe in energy, feel it move up your legs, filling your body with energy. As you breathe out, you will complete a continuous loop of energy, increasing energy with each breathing cycle.

The hands and arms are the last cycle. Visualize bringing energy into the palms of your hands, up your arms, and into your body. You will soon feel a tingling in the palms of your hands as they become alive with energy and the energy spreads through the body. Do this for as many breaths as you wish.

Once again, return to the energy loop of the spine, breathing in "strength" and breathing out "grace." Conclude the exercise by returning your mind to the frontal brain, and think about the successful, enjoyable, and creative day you're going to have.

With practice, you'll be able to generate energy with your mind whenever you need an immediate boost. Guided meditation through a master teacher is similar and can also provide energy, such as the heart chakra meditation with the sutras of peace, harmony, laughter, and love.

There are several other ways to use your mind to create energy. To begin, adopt a positive approach to everything you do. Train yourself to see the good in all things. This approach frees your mind of unproductive energy and wasted negative thoughts.

Second, develop intense confidence in yourself and everyone else. You'll find that confidence can give you energy because you'll see positive outcomes instead of negative obstacles. Having confidence in others and having no judgment about them will also give you energy.

Third, use visualizations. Visualize success – what does success look like for you? Visualize eating the right types of foods. Visualize working with high-energy, positive people. Visualize reaching your goals. Visualize having healthy cells throughout your body.

Fourth, use compassion to generate energy. Tibetan monks who spend their lives meditating about compassion radiate peace that can be felt by everyone near them. Be compassionate toward yourself, especially if you've made mistakes and bad decisions. It's healthy to go beyond your mistakes. Count the "no's" as a way of getting more "yeses." Practice being compassionate toward others, especially when they make mistakes.

Fifth, learn to widen the use of your brainwave activity while awake, moving beyond the standard 14-cycle per second beta brainwave frequency. Learn to use the profound and slower 10-cycle per second alpha brainwaves and 7-cycle per second theta brainwaves.

The beta brainwaves are used during our typical waking day. They help us perform our routine of eating, walking, driving, working, and conducting other daily tasks.

Alpha brainwaves are slower and occur during light sleep, rapid eye movement sleep or REM sleep, and during dreams. Learning to be in the alpha brainwave state while awake enables you to use it to your benefit, either by traditional sitting meditation or with eyes open, as I prefer. You have experienced these alpha waves while you're awake and may not have realized it. These brainwaves are the ones that give you a calm, soothing feeling. You may experience them while hiking in the mountains, during a slow jog, shoveling snow, raking leaves on a cool fall day, or even having an enjoyable conversation.

You can learn to use alpha brainwaves to produce energy. Some people have this ability naturally. For most people, meditation is needed to achieve this state. I prefer the eyes-open method by using meditation techniques with my eyes open peering at the distance in a detached manner. After learning how to create alpha brainwaves with the mind, the ability to achieve this state can be done on a moment's notice. In addition to a calming effect, the alpha rhythm can be used as a source of creativity since the mind is free of internal chatter.

The alpha brainwave state is being intensely studied, and new benefits are being discovered. For example, alpha brainwave meditation may increase telomerase activity. This is the enzyme that is also increased by a balanced dietary omega-3/omega-6 ratio. It's the enzyme that naturally decreases with age and is responsible for rebuilding the ends of the telomeres. Every cell in our body is constantly being replaced. The telomeres are the protective ends of the chromosomes, but they become shorter with each cell division and eventually become so short, the cell dies. A healthy amount of telomerase will prevent this shortening and prolong cell life. Alpha brainwaves can sustain a healthy amount of telomerase.

Theta brainwaves are even slower than alpha brainwaves. They occur during sleep, but it's possible to create theta brainwaves while awake through the same meditation method as alpha-brainwave creation by meditating more deeply, which requires more practice.

—

Let's return to Dave and Kate. Could they use their minds to create energy?

Dave had a habit of always seeing problems in everything around him. This was good because he could see problems before anyone else; but this tendency developed into its own major problem because his thinking contributed to feeling depressed.

"Someone at work told me today that I couldn't say three sentences without talking about a problem or about someone at work," Dave said reluctantly. "That was harsh."

"Try to change your thinking," Kate said.

"What are you talking about?" Dave asked.

"Negative thinking takes over during adult life by negative conditioning," Kate explained. "This doesn't occur in children, they think in positive ways. So, you need to recondition and retrain your mind to generate positive thoughts, or at least stop yourself from dwelling on negative thoughts."

"And before you start defending yourself by saying, "I can't change," here's a fact: everyone can change. And change will make a huge difference," Kate said convincingly. "Dave, constantly bombarding yourself with negative thoughts is depressing."

"I recall someone at work telling me something about the neurolinguistic loop," Dave said. "I wonder if this is related to my depressing thinking."

"I think it is," Kate said. "I read something about neurolinguistics. It has to do with the effect of your own words on the brain causing emotional or physical reactions. Negative thinking sets up an unhealthy negative neurolinguistic loop, which means the relentless negative words can actually create a negative neuropathway for depression."

"How do you change?"

"You change by consciously eliminating negative thoughts and replacing them with neutral or positive thoughts. Become aware of your thoughts until you learn to decrease the frequency and intensity of negative thoughts with the ultimate goal of eliminating them."

"I'll try it," Dave said.

Over time, Dave practiced being aware of his thinking and was slowly able to replace his negative thoughts with neutral or positive thinking. Seeing the good in all things was a huge help for him. One morning over a healthy weekend brunch, Dave brought up the subject of breathing.

"I just learned something new."

"What?" Kate asked.

"I learned that you can combine using your mind and your breathing for two huge benefits."

"What do you mean?"

"You can create energy and relieve stress."

"I remember learning about how breathing helps with the pain of delivery in our pregnancy class," Kate said, "but, I didn't know you can use breathing to create energy, though."

"Try it," Dave replied. "Breathe in the energy that surrounds us and create a loop of energy from the bottom of your spine to the top of your head. Breathe in, sending energy from the top of your head to the bottom of your spine. Then breathe out, sending energy from the bottom of your spine to the top of your head."

"That's easy enough."

"You can also say to yourself 'strength' while breathing in and 'grace' while breathing out," Dave said. "It gives you balance."

"Sounds good, it almost seems too simple to work."

"It takes practice," Dave said. "I did this during a run the other day and it turned the run into a pleasant experience."

"So can you use breathing to relieve acute stress?" Kate asked.

"It's easy and it creates energy too," Dave said. "Use two or three belly breaths. Put your hand over your belly button, breathe in, moving your hand up. That's all there is to it."

"Hmm," Kate said. "It's tricky. It feels like the opposite of normal breathing, but it has a calming effect."

"I like to use it before giving a big presentation," Dave said. "The other calming effect is equally breathing in and breathing out, without making a sound. Do this for several minutes whenever you're stressed. It's calming."

"Okay," Kate said, "now it's my turn to share something with you."

"Do you know what alpha brainwaves are?"

"No idea."

"Well, first of all, there are five brainwave patterns that include alpha, beta, theta, delta, and gamma."

"Sounds like Greek to me," Dave snickered with his cliché.

"Stay with me," Kate said, "beta brainwaves occur during the typical day-to-day brain activity, like getting dressed, driving, eating, and working. Gamma brainwaves are fast, 25 to 100 cycles per second with an average of 40 cycles per second. There's a theory that gamma brainwaves occur in athletes when they're in the 'zone' and play above anyone else."

"Is that what's going on when I have one of those great days closing a huge sale without even thinking about it?" Dave asked.

"Maybe. It doesn't happen much, but it's a thrill when it does!" Kate exclaimed. "The other three brain waves are related to sleep. Two are exceptional because everyone can learn to use them while awake. It should be taught in school."

"What are they?"

"They're the alpha and theta brainwaves," Kate said. "Alpha brainwaves are 7 to 10 cycles per second and slower than the waking beta brainwaves at 14 cycles per second. They occur during REM sleep, you know, rapid eye movement sleep when you're dreaming."

"So that's why you say you're dreaming if I wake you up when your eyes are quickly moving back and forth," Dave said, and that's alpha brainwave activity?"

"The exciting part is that you can go into the alpha brainwave state while you're awake," said Kate.

"I think that happens when we run together," Dave said. "After two or three miles of running, we're both floating in space talking about pleasant things and in sort of a dreamy state."

"Exactly, that's alpha brainwave time," Kate said. "It's pleasant and relaxing. Sitting meditation is the traditional way of experiencing alpha brainwaves while awake, and continues to be the best method, and you can even learn to do this with your eyes open while doing non-intense activities. It's the creative state of mind; you can come up with creative and useful ideas while in this state."

"I had no idea meditation was so powerful," Dave said. "To be honest, I thought it was a waste of time."

"I thought so too," Kate said, "but I was wrong. Not only can you experience life-changing creative ideas, but the prolonged alpha rhythm waking state has health benefits that are continuously being discovered."

"Okay, you've convinced me about the alpha brainwaves," Dave said. "Now what about the theta ones?"

"They're even more interesting," Kate said. "These are slow, like 5 cycles per second and occur while you're sound asleep. But recently it's been found that you can also create the theta brainwave state through deep meditation."

"Yeah?"

"The body has an vast ability to heal itself if we just create an environment for it to happen," Kate said. "The theta waves that occur during sleep may have some healing effect, but the theta brainwave state while awake has a strong healing effect."

"Wonderful information, Kate," Dave said. "I'm going to try both of them."

"Incidentally, delta brainwaves occur during profoundly deep sleep and are slow, at about 3 cycles per second," Kate said. "The key thing about delta brainwaves is that you have to have at least 15 minutes of this deep sleep each night, or else psychological health will deteriorate. Scientists awakened people during this delta brainwave sleep time for several consecutive nights and began seeing psychological changes. We need the deep delta brainwave sleep time."

# 7

# Stress Control as an Energy Source

**You can increase your energy level** by managing your stress. We deal with stress every day. Surprisingly, acute stress doesn't hurt anyone. The human system has evolved over thousands of years to manage acute stress with the appropriate amount of stress-response hormones and neurotransmitters.

However, chronic stress can cause life-threatening health problems and drain energy. To counteract this, you can learn about chronic stress, the opposite of acute stress, and manage it. Recognize you're in a chronic stress situation such as caring for an emotionally-demanding family member, or working in an over-controlled, demanding workplace environment. Change from concentrating on problems to searching for positive events and solutions. Obtain eight hours of sleep each night and do one hour of vigorous exercise each day.

In a discussion of stress and energy, the concept of happiness needs to be reviewed to gain a more complete picture. About 10% of happiness is from life's conditions such as getting married, getting a raise, buying a house. These are wonderful events and provide a new level of happiness; however, these events are usually fleeting, lasting hours, months, or even three to five years for marriage, yet most people return to their baseline level of happiness over time.

Genetics accounts for 50% of your happiness level. Look at babies. You can determine their lifetime level of happiness by simple observation. Some are smiling and active. Others are irritable and nervous.

The good news is that you're in charge of the remaining 40% of your happiness level. It's your behavior and you can manage it. People who sustain a high-level of happiness focus on what's internally important to them. This means spending time doing what they enjoy – their life's calling, their passion, spending time with family and friends, and being involved in the community. People who maintain high-level happiness live in and savor the moment.

Let's resume our discussion about stress since this can have an impact not only on happiness, but also on health and energy. Acute stress is not an issue. People have faced acute stress, lasting minutes to a few hours, since prehistoric times and have learned to adapt without causing injury. When a stressful situation develops such as having a near accident or being late for a meeting, the heart rate increases, the breathing rate increases, and you feel stressed, but these are fleeting events, and you soon return to your daily routine once the stressor passes.

Not so with chronic stress. Humans have not adapted well from the ancient world to our new world environment, and three reasons for chronic stress have emerged.

First, we live in a widely different environment than our prehistoric ancestors. We live in cities, we race through the day in our automobiles, fly from one city to another in hours, and we are now highly dependent on electronics, cellphones, and computers, all setting us up for the chronic stress of rushing to make deadlines and meetings, competing for space, and unexpected breakdowns and delays.

Second, we almost always experience delayed return in everything we do, and without guarantee of success. We work for hours, weeks, months, and sometimes years doing things that have no immediate return. For example, a farmer plants, weeds, and harvests all for the future, yet faces the possibility of crop failure at any time. Graduate students work for years not knowing if they will obtain their degree or if they'll find the job of their dreams after earning that degree. We hope for the return of our efforts later, sometimes in a few weeks but often in many years, and this creates chronic, and sometimes severe, ongoing stress.

Third, we need the feeling of being in control. In reality, most events are beyond our control. We personally cannot do anything to control the lion's share of situations, but we think we can because of technology available to us resulting in chronic stress.

The stress response varies widely among people because stress is the physical and emotional response to a person's interpretation of an event or threat. Stress is a fear-based reaction. A plane ride with up and down loops is exhilarating for some, producing healthy neurotransmitters and hormones, but terrifying for others, producing stress hormones and chemicals.

There are two parts to the stress response: the event and the person's perceived ability to cope with the event. For example, some people put themselves in stressful situations all the time, such as starting new companies or running for public office, because they know they can cope with them, while others interpret trivial situations such as going to a social gathering or meeting new people as stressful because they feel they can't cope with them.

What are some ideas for coping with stress? There are several. The happiness factor is important, learn to focus on what's intrinsically important and discarding or ignoring everything else.

People who are better able to cope with stress are self-compassionate. This means treating yourself with kindness and forgiveness when bad things happen, especially when it's your own fault. Be kind to yourself and forgive yourself.

Use breathing for stress relief. Take a few belly breaths. Use the equal-in and equal-out breathing technique. You can do this for several minutes. It has a calming effect on the vagal nerve system. Using this technique, you can also gain a huge amount of Level-10 Energy by using your mind to deeply breathe in the energy from a point at the very beginning of the universe and breathing out the energy to the exact same point.

You can also eliminate stress by realizing that it is your interpretation of a threat, based on fear. When we eliminate the fear, we eliminate the stress.

# 8

# Conquer Fear for a Lifesaving Source of Energy

**The positive emotions** include joy, gratitude, love, pride, and serenity. The negative ones include fear, anger, sadness, guilt, and shame. Frustration is a combination of emotions. Why do you need to be reminded of these emotions? The easy answer is that positive ones create energy and negative ones use up energy.

Yet there's a deep, profound reason for understanding the emotions: fear and anger are so powerful that they can actually destroy life. Conquering these emotions offers the greatest opportunity for creating an energy-filled, exciting life.

Consider two groups of people who are similar in age, background, weight, and who are outwardly healthy. Both groups exercise, yet people in the first could have a heart attack, but in the second group, none are at risk. How is this possible? Exercise prevents heart attacks. People in the first group exercise out of fear of having a heart attack. They're angry about being to forced exercise. They trudge through exercise every day and complain the whole time. The second group? They *love* to exercise. They enjoy it. They look forward to how it feels. It creates energy, it improves muscle tone and posture, it activates the feel-good neurotransmitters, and as a bonus, it allows them to see their friends. Nobody in this group is going to have a heart attack.

People in the first group are doing "fear-based" exercise. The fear of a heart attack is so great that it produces cortisol and other damaging chemicals that far outweigh the benefits of exercise. The solution is to learn to enjoy exercise and feel the benefits. It'll give you a Level-10 Energy Day, and it could possibly save your life.

Fear-based actions occur in many other areas of our lives, most of the time unknowingly. Here's another example: two groups of people eat the same foods, yet some will develop diabetes, hypertension, and heart disease. Why? They're forcing themselves to eat "healthy foods" and are filled with anger and chronic stress about having to eat foods they don't like. They're trying so hard to not eat too much, that the cortisol and other toxic chemicals produced by these emotions cancel the benefits of healthy eating. People in the other group, however, love to eat healthy foods. They enjoy finding foods that have healthy protein, omega-3 fatty acids, and slow-burn carbs. They learn to love the taste. Most of all, they enjoy the feeling that the food is not going to hurt them and will provide energy. You can teach yourself to enjoy choosing healthy foods and savor the taste.

Another example: two groups of people have the same job, and some will develop hypertension and heart disease. You know these people. They dread going to work on Monday, struggle through the day and incessantly complain about the job. They're the people who are angry about having to work, and yet are in constant fear of not working. They can't wait for 5 o'clock so they can escape the drudgery that they have created for themselves. This chronic stress, anger, and fear culminate in deadly levels of cortisol release and toxic-reaction chemicals day in and day out, causing hypertension and heart disease. People in the second group, however, love their jobs. They look forward to going to work; it gives them energy. They enjoy meeting the challenges, talking to people, and they enjoy the workday. Even if they are not naturally experiencing their passion and their life's calling, these people learn to find a way to enjoy their work.

Regardless of the job, it can become enjoyable. My friend Marco was in his 20s and worked at the carwash making minimum wage, and he loved it. I saw him there for years. He was always smiling and had a quick, friendly hello and made light, pleasant conversation with the customers. For him, he didn't go to work at a carwash. He went to a place to talk to people. He loved to see people and speak with them. He was doing his most favorite thing: talking to people! Over time, he started his own car-detailing business and is in the process of growing it to include several car-detailing outlets. He's on his way to huge financial success and a healthy energetic life. He never thought of this while working at the carwash. Because of his attitude, opportunities developed, and he had a ton of energy. He learned to find a way to see enjoyment and create energy in his job.

---

Overcoming fear can save your life. To do so, you must know that the body can heal itself. Let's talk to Buck about his experience. He is a successful entrepreneur, busy husband, and father of three children. He was training for a triathlon and had a good workout but overdid it. He built up too much lactic acid from anaerobic metabolism, too much muscle fatigue, and developed a rapid heart rate.

"So, what happened, Buck?" the interviewer asked.

"The heart rate didn't slow down after my shower and it kept going at a rate of 135 beats per minute for a couple of hours."

"What'd you do?"

"I went to the cardiologist, who was able to bring it back to my normal rate of 58 with a cardioversion shock," Buck said nonchalantly. "At first I denied anything happened and returned to my training, but I became so nervous, I couldn't work out."

"What do you mean by nervous?"

"I'd never been afraid of anything before, but I was afraid that if I worked out too much, the out-of-control rapid heart rate would start again. I feared I would be limited by my heart. I couldn't live that way. I go full-out or not at all. I was afraid my life would be shortened. I became afraid of the future."

"Sounds scary. What happened?"

"I was working out a few weeks ago and had a panic attack after my heart rate doubled, which was safe enough, but I didn't know if it was the good rate or the bad rate. Fear gripped me so bad that I had to stop and make sure my heart rate returned to normal. It was frustrating and created a vicious cycle of fear by not doing enough exercise, which created more fear, which generated more fear again."

"You were heading for trouble. What'd you do?"

"It took a while, but I finally realized that fear was doing a huge amount of damage and that I had to eliminate it or go on living at half speed, an unacceptable option."

"How'd you do it?"

"I thought that now that I recognized the problem it was going to be easy. All I needed to do was to build my confidence back up one day at a time by running a little more, swimming longer, and slowly lifting more weights to prove to myself that my heart could build back up to normal. But it didn't work. The fear continued to cause episodes of extra beats. It was worse than ever."

"What happened next?"

"I tried something else. I used will power, telling myself over and over that I had no fear. That didn't work at all. I kept having skipped heart beats and had to slow down, which made the situation worse. It wasn't like a broken bone that heals in six weeks and is stronger than ever. This was a heart problem that was only going to recur and get worse. This fear generated a huge outpouring of toxic chemicals causing all types of problems, especially an increased heart rate."

"You tried the recommended methods, but they failed. So what'd you do next?"

"I believe that there are always options. I had to keep exploring them. I learned that the body has a huge ability to heal itself. I just needed to find out how. For me, it was through meditation and using theta brainwaves along with attention and visualization."

"Sounds interesting. Please tell me more."

"Theta brainwaves are the slow ones that occur during sleep and have some effect on health while sleeping. But by creating the theta-brainwave state while awake through meditation, healing can take place. Once in the theta state, I focused my attention on the heart muscle, the heart arteries, and the heart electrical system by reprogramming the DNA back 20 to 30 years when my heart was healthy.

"How's that possible?"

"The DNA has many built-in repair systems that keep the DNA the same as it was at birth. All of our cells continually renew themselves, so during the next cell-growth division cycle, I reprogrammed them to renew themselves as they were 20 or 30 years ago. It's also important to eliminate the memory of the inciting event from the cells as they are renewed so the new cells have no memory of the shock causing the event."

"Did you try it?"

"Yes, as soon as I realized that my heart could return to being normal and healthy, the fear vanished. Now it had become like a broken bone; over a six-month period, it would heal and then be as strong as before. Therefore, I could continue working out at full speed, not overdoing it, and not be limited by a heart problem. All of the fear completely vanished, because the reason for the fear was eliminated. The fear-based life was gone."

"Did it work?"

"Yes, beyond my wildest dreams. I no longer have any fear about my heart. It's strong, healthy, and will keep me going at full speed for a long, long time. It's a great feeling."

---

You too can transform fear, anger, and stress into positive energy.

---

Let me share a story about Michael. He's a Level-10 Energy guy. I was a guest on his radio show. He told me he had developed lung cancer, which had spread to his heart. He took the news as anyone would, as a death sentence. He feared the upcoming surgery. He feared that his life was cut short. He feared he would have to leave his family. He feared no longer being able to do his life's work. He feared death. The list of fears went on and on. This is a normal and expected response.

But the normal response stopped there. Somewhere in the back of his mind and for a reason unknown to him, he understood clearly that he wanted to be fit and strong for the lung surgery, so he increased his exercise program. Suddenly, after working up a profuse sweat, his heart pounding, and his breath coming fast, Michael's fear of death vanished. And all the other fears vanished too. He underwent the surgery with profound success. He had no chemotherapy and no radiation. He was cured. That was eight years ago. Today he continues to be grateful for every minute of the day and enjoys life to the fullest.

# 9

# Social Interaction Pays Big Benefits

**Do you know people** who can instantly charge your battery? Being near them, talking to them, and interacting with them energize you. Stay with them. They're good for your health. Better yet, become one yourself and spread the energy.

—

Hans and Nell were a depressing couple. Somehow, they had managed to find each other and connect. Ask Hans how he was doing, and he would reply kiddingly, "Not bad for a dead man." He found something negative in everything, and usually commented on it. Nell was the same way. She instantly found something negative about every event. Ask her about attending a celebration, and she'll tell you that it was no fun because there were too many people. A holiday trip would turn into one complaint and problem after another. The wait for the plane was too long, there was no food on the plane, the taxi ride to the hotel was too expensive, the room wasn't ready, it was raining, it was too hot, it was too cold. Her mind filled with so many negative thoughts and complaints, she completely missed the beautiful scenery and interesting people around her. And if the couple entered a room together, you can be sure they drained energy from everyone around them.

Not so with Coe and Jill. Coe always had an upbeat hello for everyone and he made people feel special. He didn't dwell on the negative things about people or ideas. Jill had a sparkling personality. She smiled all the time. She had a special ability to find something positive about everyone she met during the day. She would compliment salespeople on their friendly service or their smile or their clothing. She talked to people at restaurants as if they were lifelong friends. She didn't fear kids; she found out what they liked and lit up their day. When Coe and Jill entered a room, they filled it with energy for everyone around them.

---

You know these types of people. You may not be able to be Coe and Jill and probably wouldn't want to be this extreme, but their basic approach to life is positive, enjoyable, and worthy of emulation.

The science behind the transfer of energy between people seems to indicate a relationship between the social activity and the feel-good neurotransmitters. These include phenylethylamine or PEA, which increases the activity of other neurotransmitters such as dopamine, which gives the feeling of pleasure; norepinephrine, which is a stimulator; acetylcholine, for improved mental activity; and especially serotonin, which can regulate impulse control preventing hostile interaction. PEA is highly concentrated in the limbic system, or the emotional center of the brain, which increases motivation and feelings. Oxytocin is also involved as the bonding hormone neurotransmitter.

Community can give you energy and health. For example, over 100 years ago, a group of individuals came to the United States from a small village in Italy. They settled in the same Pennsylvania location and stayed in the small town for generations. They were similar to people in surrounding villages. They ate the same foods, they did the same amount of exercise, and they had the same types of jobs. However, no one under the age of 65 there had a heart attack, but a high percentage of people in the surrounding villages did. Why?

The only difference found between the two groups was their amount of community trust. Over many generations, members of this community built a huge amount of trust among themselves. Everyone knew they could count on other community members to help them if they had problems or trouble. No one in the community would hurt anyone, and they all forgave each other. Neighbors would always try to help as much as they could.

As a result, the stress level was extremely low compared to that of surrounding towns. People knew they could find help from the community, which eliminated a major stressor in their lives. As a result, there was no chronic stress, no cortisol response, healthy hearts, and increased energy.

How can you become an energy producer? It's easy. All you need to do to start is to create your Level-10 Energy Days. This will produce enough energy to share among your friends and your community. Help people, have compassion for people, and do not judge yourself or anyone else.

# 10

# Your Job is a Springboard for Energy

**Does your job** take all the energy you have? You can actually turn work into an energy builder. Some people are able to do this naturally. For most, however, it's a learned response. The good news is that almost everyone, no matter the job they do, can learn to create energy while working.

How is it possible to gain energy from a job? You walk into the office or store or factory, and you're instantly faced with people who start using up your energy. Your boss has extra work for you and throws in a negative comment about last week's project. Your first sale involves somebody complaining about the product, or worse complaining about you. Your supervisor gives you a team of workers who are lazy. This all occurs in the first 15 minutes after you arrive, and the day continues on the same path for the next eight to ten hours. All of these situations require your energy, and there's nothing left at the end of the day for you or for your family.

Yet it's possible to gain energy during the workday. The best way is to start with a huge amount of energy through the required amount of sleep, exercise, and the three energy-producing foods. Concentrate on positive events. Shrug off negative comments and events, let them pass through you without using energy to judge them or fight them. Finally, gain energy through positive interactions with people and focus on successes, no matter how small.

Create energy by doing work that's aligned with your character and your passion. If you are doing work you love and you're passionate about, three things happen. First, it's not work and you enjoy it. Second, you're good at it. And, third, there's no real competition because your work is unique, and no one else has the same personality or the same approach as you.

So make a genuine effort to find your talents and passion. Talents are recurrent behaviors and activities that you enjoy doing every day and keep returning to over the years. Know and study them. There are internet resources available to confirm your three to five talents among the more than 30 identifiable specific talents. Apply them to a job or create a work environment that will use these talents. There are always ways to make money and use your talents on a daily basis.

For example, if you have a passion for numbers, balancing the books can be the biggest thrill of the day for you. This is a talent. That's what you should do because it will be non-stressful, easy to do, and will produce an unbelievable amount of energy. When your work is aligned with your personality, this is truly a blessing.

If you have a talent and a passion for music or art, learn how to create a work situation that will allow you to do this all day and provide a source of income. Turning this into reality is no small task, and becoming an entrepreneur in whatever way it takes to translate your vision into actuality is a huge endeavor. However, there are teachers, mentors, programs, and unlimited resources that can assist in this process. The reward in terms of energy and enjoyment is worth the expended effort.

Do you have a job doing the same routine day in and day out to make money so you can do what you love to do after work hours? Don't let it take all of your energy. When you put some energy into your job, you'll receive Level-10 Energy in return. Use your personality. Find a new way of doing things. Volunteer for extra work. Help someone. Start early. Stay late. Three things will happen. The job will be more enjoyable. You're more likely to be given a promotion and a raise. And, you'll increase your energy so much that you'll go beyond this job and obtain a new job that you love and that pays twice as much.

Marcia had an entry-level job of double-checking numbers for a financial company, potentially extremely tedious and boring. However, she had taken an internet-based, self-analytical series of questions to determine her specific talents. She found that she was highly capable of three-dimensional thinking, and one of her talents was referred to as analytical. She applied these findings to her job. She developed an intricately, interconnected spreadsheet program that decreased the time for preparing quarterly reports from three days to three hours. This was such a huge advance that her salary was doubled, and her software program opened the potential for a royalty-based income stream.

Find and create work that will utilize your talents. Your passion for the work will energize your life.

---

Let's talk about Lance. One morning he walked into work, and said, "Hi Alice, how's it going?"

"Not good," Alice replied gloomily. "My dog ate my new shoes last night."

"That's too bad," Lance said on his way to his office, where someone was waiting for him.

"That product you sold me yesterday is no longer working," the customer told him before he even sat down. "What do I do?"

"Talk to the service department at the end of the hall," Lance said. "They'll fix it.

Alice, my email isn't working. Is yours?"

"Yes, mine's good."

"I'll have to call the helpline," Lance muttered, and then spent 30 minutes on hold and more time having someone go through the steps to restore his email. In the meantime, the phone kept ringing and messages piled up. By now his energy was gone, and it had only been the first hour of the day.

---

In contrast, let's find out how Susie's day went. She started the day after an excellent night of sleep and a great class with her morning dance workout group. She was energized to start the workday.

"Hi Sam. You're looking good this morning," Susie said as she walked into the office.

"I'm not feeling good; my dog ate one of my new shoes," Sam said in a cranky voice.

"I'm sorry, but that sounds like a funny story," Susie said smiling. "What kind of dog do you have and how'd it happen?"

"He thought we were playing," Sam said. "I turned my back for five minutes, and he destroyed my shoe. I guess you're right, it was funny now that you mention it."

"Sounds like a great dog; you should bring the trouble-maker to the office," Susie said as she went to her office with a little more energy because she was able to improve someone's day.

"Oh, you're already here to start the day?" Susie said to John, who was sitting in the chair.

"That product you sold me yesterday isn't working," John said with annoyance.

"Not a problem, we can fix it," Susie said with a friendly hello and shook John's hand. "We have an friendly guy in our service department who can solve that problem for you immediately. Let's go see him."

They walked down the hall to the service department and the problem was fixed right away. John loved the product and was excited to have it permanently repaired.

"I'll be back to see you again," John told Susie as he bounded out of the office.

Once again Susie gained a little more positive energy as she said goodbye to John. Her extra help paid big dividends in increased sales for the company and also provided an extra boost of energy for her.

"Sam, is your email working?" Susie asked after returning to the office. "Mine seems to be acting up."

"No, mine's working just fine," Sam said. "Can I help you?"

"No, it's a nuisance, but I'll call the helpline," Susie said as she punched in the numbers of her hands-free headphone. She went through the automated selections and a series of phone numbers, writing them down in case the call was disconnected.

"How are you today?" Susie asked. "You seem to be working long hours."

"I'm good, thank you. How can I help?"

"I'm not able to receive or send any emails this morning," Susie said.

"We will be pleased to fix that for you. What's your name, account number, username, password?"

"I'm Susie and I don't have any of that information, but I have a simple request that I'm sure you can help me with," she said in an upbeat tone.

"Check your cable going into the router box near your desk."

"Whoa, look at this," Susie said excitedly. "The cable is disconnected; it must have accidentally become unhinged during office cleaning last night."

"Problem fixed. Thank you very much for your time and your help," Susie said. "You're going to have a great day."

The first hour of the day came to an end, and Suzie had more energy than when she started. The remaining part of the day would continue to give her energy.

Your job can be a source of energy if you approach the workday by searching for ways to improve other people's day.

Look for the good things at work, compliment people, help others, and let the negative events at the workplace pass through you without registering a loss of energy.

# 11

# Feel the Energy with Music

**Have you ever heard music** that gives you energy? You may have and didn't know it. Think about it, if you have, listen to that music right now for confirmation, and for a quick boost of energy.

Certain types of music can produce the feel-good neurotransmitters such as endorphins. To show that music can create a positive feeling, people have been given an anti-endorphin substance, and they experienced no improved feeling.

The brain, the body, and all the cells vibrate at differing frequencies. Some types of music will cause a paired vibration resulting in energy. This is called entrainment, which means matching vibration. If five pendulum clocks are all set at different starting points, within four hours, the pendulum of each clock will swing at the same time in synchronous timing. Music can also function to entrain the cyclic pattern of your brain in the same manner.

Music provides an entry point into different regions of the brain. The pitch, harmony, rhythm, and emotion components of music each reach a specific part of the brain. For example, for individuals who have an injury to a specific part of the brain, music can create an alternate pathway to make the region functional. Music therapy such as choral singing and rhythmic body movements can improve muscle coordination and behavioral function in Parkinson's disease.

Music can change the brain and create plasticity, which means new brain-cell neuropathway growth. After several weeks of learning to play the piano, the region of the brain involved in this activity becomes larger and more connected. Learning this new skill has rewired the brain.

Music can add a huge amount of energy during exercise, such as running, cycling, or group activities like spinning, aerobics, Zumba, or body pump classes. For example, a song like Bob Seger's "Fire Inside" can provide a perfect downbeat for the right or left foot while running on the treadmill at a certain speed. The musical beat directly provides a pathway to a specific region of the brain for improved motor efficiency and energy.

The same effect occurs among people in spin and other aerobic classes where music is played. The first song is generally slow tempo for warm-up. The middle songs are high tempo, which provide an excellent cadence for the right or left foot, and the speed can be doubled for extra work. The last song is for cool-down with a slow rhythm. Music allows individuals in the class to create a cadence that produces group Level-10 Energy that can be shared by everyone.

All types of music can provide energy, and an up-tempo rhythmic beat is usually best, but a triumphant symphony such as Beethoven's Egmont Overture can provide the same energy. Mozart's music can provide the feeling of a soaring eagle.

People vary in their response to music. Some music will have the opposite of the expected effect. For example, a beautifully played Verdi's Requiem can completely drain energy in some people yet lift the spirits of others.

# 12

# Quick Bursts of Energy and Level-10 Energy for Life

**Find yourself with low energy?** There are some tricks you can use for a quick boost of energy. Most are common-sense actions, but some of them may be new to you. Learn the list and use a trick or two to overcome your next low-energy moment.

Help someone. This doesn't have to be dramatic. Help somebody find their car, find their papers, find a parking spot, shovel snow, organize a birthday party, make a repair, or recover from a personal setback. The simpler, the better. It's the simple step that will give you a quick burst of energy.

Stand up. Surprisingly, standing will give you energy. Stand while you're talking to someone, stand while you work for a few minutes, and especially stand while you talk on the telephone. Standing triggers muscle groups for an extra boost of energy.

Compliment someone. This is easy to do. Compliment someone on their positive attitude, a job well done, providing a good answer or solution, or wearing uplifting clothes. The right compliment is two for one;

not only does it provide a quick burst of energy for you, but it also energizes the other person as well.

Make a sale or close a deal. Big or small, it'll give you energy. You've worked hard to find a client, give your pitch, respond to objections, and close. You sign the deal, shake hands, and make the money. This is pure energy.

Call a positive client. You've had call after call, rejection after rejection. It's time to call a positive client. Just to talk. It'll give you energy.

Take a cold shower. This is how you do it. First use comfortable warm water going down your neck and back. Gradually turn the dial to cold and let it run down your spine for a few seconds. Then turn it back to warm for a few seconds. Repeat this three to five times, and you'll trigger an energy response. Your eyes will be wide open and your skin will be tingling.

Try this one. Plug your feet into the ground for energy. You're giving a speech or meeting an important person. Stand with your back straight, head up and chin in, and step with one foot onto the floor as if it is an unlimited source of energy. Now move your other foot forward standing on the source of energy. Both feet are on the floor, one slightly in front of the other, then take a big diaphragmatic breath bringing in the energy. You can feel it. It gives your body energy, your voice energy, and your mind energy.

Drink water for a quick boost of energy. Find your mind wondering, developing a food craving, sleepy? Drink some water.

Warm sesame oil massage can give you wonderful energy. The skin is filled with immune response cells and energy growth factors. A message will stimulate and energize the skin and your body.

Looking good will give you energy. Clothes and colors that fit your personality will give you energy. Find out what they are, talk to an expert. Stand tall with a straight back and square shoulders with an upbeat erect posture for energy. Smiling gives you energy because other people will respond in a positive way.

Laughter, a distinct human behavior, will provide energy. This is especially true if the laugh is about a positive story. Laughing at other people's expense is an energy loss.

There are hundreds of other sources of energy, both big and small. Discover your own. When you do, share them, creating even more energy. Bursts of energy can keep your life vital and strong.

Create Level-10 Energy Days for life. It's the feeling of being on top of the world with no worries. It's the feeling of doing anything you want without stress. It's the feeling of unlimited creativity. It's the feeling of enjoying every minute of the day. It's the best feeling in the world. It's a way of life.

Concluding with quick facts to live by: Eight hours of sleep. One hour of exercise every day at the best of your ability. Eat the right three foods for energy including lean protein, omega-3 fatty acids, and slow-burn carbs. Learn something new every day and keep learning. Spend introspection time using alpha and theta brainwaves for mind-body balance, creativity, and healing. Manage chronic stress. Make time for social and community interaction. Make your job a springboard for energy. Find your music for energy. Keep looking good as a source of energy. Be grateful and help people for energy.

---

You are in charge. You control your energy.
You can do this better than anyone else.
Your chance of success is unlimited.
Fuel for life: Level-10 Energy

# About the Author

**Dr. Gary Epler** is an internationally-known pulmonary and critical care professor at Harvard Medical School in Boston. He has written four health books in the critically-acclaimed "You're the Boss" series about people taking charge of their health and disease including *Manage Your Disease*, *BOOP*, *Asthma*, and *Food: You're the Boss*.

Dr. Epler discovered the treatable lung disorder bronchiolitis obliterans organizing pneumonia (BOOP). He found a new parasite in South America, chronicled the nutritional needs of North African children, and managed the tuberculosis refugee program in Southeast Asia.

In addition to conducting clinical and research work, Dr. Epler strives to educate. He became editor-in-chief of an internet-based educational program in critical care and pulmonary medicine offered by the American College of Chest Physicians. *Business Week* acclaimed him for his development of e-health educational programs that enable patients to manage their health and diseases. Dr. Epler has been recognized yearly from 1994 to 2013 in "The Best Doctors in America" and recognized as one of *Boston Magazine's* "2007 Top Doctors in Town."

Dr. Epler has run seven marathons including those in Boston and New York; he proposed to his wife, Joan, at the start of the Paris Marathon. For their first anniversary, they ran the original Greek marathon together. He delivered the 20th baby from a mother who named the baby after him. He's been one of the Boston Celtics team doctors. He has taught medicine throughout the world and was fortunate enough to save a dying infant in South America from an overwhelming parasitic infection by using the sap from a fig tree. He saved a baby who choked on a donut during a little league baseball game he was coaching. He is active in the community. He coached soccer, basketball, hockey, baseball, and club baseball at Boston College. He lives in the Boston area with his wife, Joan.